EFFECT MATTERS

How Reporting and Interpreting Effect Sizes Can Improve your
Publication Prospects and Make the World a Better Place!

STATISTICAL POWER TRIP

How the Analysis of Statistical Power will Help you Win Grants,
Get Published, and have a Successful Research Career!

META-ANALYSIS MADE EASY

How to Draw Definitive Conclusions from Inconclusive Studies
and Find Untapped Gold Mines for Further Research!

PAUL D. ELLIS

MadMethods 1-3

ISBN: 978-1-927230-62-6
Copyright © 2020 by Paul D. Ellis

Published by MadMethods, an imprint of KingsPress.org,
PO Box 66145, Beach Haven, Auckland 0749, New Zealand.

To get this title in other formats and to find other titles in the
MadMethods series, visit www.MadMethods.co

Version: 1.1 (September 2020)

What readers are saying about
The Essential Guide to Effect Sizes

A wonderful resource! I have read many books on research and statistical methods but few that convey the concepts as clearly as this one, and fewer still that I can say I actually enjoyed reading. I would recommend it to those who are just starting to grapple with research methods as well as the more experienced researcher.

— Carrington Shepherd

Who knew statistics was this interesting?

— Amazon Reviewer

I thoroughly enjoyed this and read it twice. Later I incorporated it into a module in my advanced stats class for doctoral students. The topic was perfect for them, and the comfortable writing style made the book a delight to read. As noted by the author–some people write to impress and others to instruct. This book is for instruction.

— Wm A. Sands

This stats reform business is serious, we all need to get into it, and Paul's book is a terrific guide. Enjoy!

— Geoff Cumming

Outstanding and easy to understand reference. Inordinately helpful.

— William Jacobson

Given the increasing recognition of the severe limitations of standard null-hypothesis significance tests, I find all three topics covered in the book important as they indicate ways how we can substantially improve the interpretation of our empirical research results. I would recommend this book to scholars, doctoral students, and practitioners interested in the advanced interpretation of empirical research findings.

— Andreas Schwab

I actually emailed friends to tell them I was excited that this book was on my summer reading list. I'm enjoying it very much. This is the clearest presentation of three very complex and important subjects: effect size, power analysis, and meta-analysis.

— Amazon Reviewer

If you want to get an overview of the issues of effect sizes, statistical power, and meta-analysis, I can think of no better book to start with.

— Amazon Reviewer

Exceptionally lucid overview of power analysis, effect sizes, and sample size calculations. Wonderful book.

— Stijn Debrouwere

Contents

EFFECT SIZE MATTERS

How Reporting and Interpreting Effect Sizes
Can Improve your Publication Prospects and
Make the World a Better Place!

PAUL D. ELLIS

Effect Size Matters:
How Reporting and Interpreting Effect Sizes Can Improve your
Publication Prospects and Make the World a Better Place!

Copyright © 2020 by Paul D. Ellis, 978-1-927230-56-5

Published by MadMethods, an imprint of KingsPress.org,
PO Box 66145, Beach Haven, Auckland 0749, New Zealand.

To get this title in other formats and to find other titles in the
MadMethods series, visit www.MadMethods.co

Image sources: "The blind men and the elephant," Wikimedia
Commons, public domain. "Jump for Joy," by Kreg Steppe,
Flickr, CC BY-SA 2.0.

Version: 1.2 (September 2020)

Dedication: For my students.

"Statistical significance is the least interesting thing about the results. You should describe the results in terms of measures of magnitude—not just, does a treatment affect people, but how much does it affect them."

— Gene Glass, quoted in Hunt (1997: 29–30)

Why do I need this book?

Science, in essence, comprises two activities: (1) discovering new stuff and (2) whacking it with a hammer to see what happens. This book is for the hammer-whackers. It's for those of us trying to figure out why things work the way they do.

If your job is to learn how some *thing* affects some other *thing,* this book is for you. Specifically, it's for those who want to know the effect of X on Y, regardless of whether we are talking about:

- the effect of a treatment on some outcome
- the effect of a strategy on performance
- the effect of a crisis on decision-making
- the effect of an intervention on addiction
- the effect of advertising on behavior
- the effect of a drug on mental health
- the effect of an innovation on standards of living
- the effect of a vaccine on the spread of a disease

Perhaps you are not used to thinking of yourself as a researcher of effects (or a hammer-whacker). I certainly didn't. Like most researchers I began my career with a tool box full of techniques for crunching data and testing hypotheses. I lived and died on the results of statistical tests. Those tools are useful, but they are just tools. They are not the main thing.

So, what is the main thing?

Whether you test hypotheses or not, whether you crunch data or don't, the main thing is to move towards a better understanding of real world effects.

An effect may be the result of a researcher's intervention or an act of nature. It could be the outcome of a plan, a process, or a collision with an iceberg. An effect may be desirable or undesirable, anticipated or surprising. It may be a one-off occurrence or it may happen every day of the week and twice on Sundays.

Effects are the stuff of life and stuff happens.

What do researchers do? We study effects. Your specific field of interest may be medicine, education, economics, communications, geography, political science, psychology, sociology, social work, management, marketing, linguistics, epidemiology, international relations, industrial relations, development studies, environmental studies, information science, or zymurgy, but you are in the business of estimating effect sizes.

Researchers estimate effect sizes in order to interpret their meaning and make sense of the world we live in.

14

In this book, you will learn these two essential skills—how to estimate and interpret effect sizes. In Part A, we will look at different ways to estimate the size of an effect; in Part B, we will look at different ways to interpret and draw conclusions from our estimates.

Five reasons to read this book

There are at least five reasons why researchers ought to be interested in effect sizes:

1. Effect sizes, not p-values, are the primary output of your study. Your estimate of the effect size constitutes your study's evidence. Since you spent months or years looking for it, it would be senseless not to report it. A study that doesn't report effect sizes is as convincing as a prosecution case with no witnesses. The prosecutor may tell a good story, but without evidence he's just wasting time. This point bears repeating: your estimate of the effect size is your evidence. Without it, your research is incomplete.

2. The estimation of effect sizes is essential to the interpretation of a study's results. Practical take-aways based on p values tend to be vague and speculative. In contrast, reporting the effect size facilitates the explicit interpretation of the substantive or practical significance of a result.

3. Reporting effect sizes prevents you re-inventing the wheel. By comparing effect size estimates obtained in different settings, researchers can better identify prospective lines of enquiry while avoiding investigative dead ends.

4. Reporting and interpreting effect sizes improves your publication prospects. Journal editors are increasingly insisting on the reporting of effect sizes in their guidelines for prospective authors. These calls are being made in every discipline, from education to rehabilitation, and from psychology to business studies. We would be wise to anticipate a future where studies that don't report effect sizes are routinely given desk rejects. Researchers who learn how to report and interpret effect sizes will benefit from these changing publication policies.

5. In many disciplines there is an ongoing push towards relevance and engagement with stakeholders beyond the research community. If our research is to make sense to practitioners and non-specialists, we need to abandon the time-worn habit of drawing large conclusions from small p values and engage directly with the evidence itself. We need to shift our focus from "did this test achieve statistical significance?" to "how big is the effect and what does it mean?" Research that makes sense will benefit society far more than

research no one reads or understands. The highly-cited researcher of tomorrow will be the one who seizes these emerging opportunities to explore new avenues of significance and meaning.

This book is not a text book. It's more of a rough and ready guide to a set of skills every researcher needs. It shouldn't take more than an hour or two to familiarize yourself with the concepts in this book.

Considering the potential returns on your investment, it will be a couple of hours well-spent.

Who wrote this book?

I'm a methods guy, but I never meant to be. As an undergrad, I found research methods and stats courses frighteningly difficult. I would get hung up on assumptions that seemed to make no sense, and I refused to be impressed by jargon.

Years later, through no fault of my own, I became a methods teacher. For 15 years I taught Research Methods to graduate student, and I enjoyed the challenge of being pushed by bright Ph.D. candidates.

At some point during this period I stumbled across effect sizes, and it was like my world turned upside-down. Or right-side up. I began to see that much of what I had been taught, and was now teaching, was incidental to the larger purposes of research. I had been taught to measure constructs and assess the veracity of hypotheses using tests of statistical significance, but I had never been taught how to estimate and interpret effect sizes.

Learning about effect sizes was the single best thing that ever happened to me as a researcher. Imagine a gold digger used to finding flakes and grains unearthing the 140 pound Welcome Stranger nugget. The fine flakes of what I had learned were still valuable; they just weren't as valuable as what I had now.

It was around about this time that I started getting recognition for my research—prizes, citations, even a medal. At one point I was rated the most prolific scholar in my field in the Asia-Pacific region. By all appearances, I was a successful scholar. But deep down, I was frustrated that I hadn't learned about effect sizes sooner.

How had I missed this?!

They say you don't learn anything until you teach it to others, so I began to pass on what I was learning about effect sizes. I began to teach meta-analysis and the analysis of statistical power in seminars. I developed the habit of reporting and interpreting effect sizes in my research papers. Serving on the editorial boards of several top tier journals, I began asking authors the same sorts of questions I was asking myself.

And then I wrote a book.

I wrote *The Essential Guide to Effect Sizes: Statistical Power, Meta-Analysis, and the Interpretation of Research Results* because I was frustrated with dense texts that struck me as unnecessarily complex and dense. It seemed that many of these books were written to impress rather than instruct. I saw an opportunity to write a jargon-free primer that covered all three legs of the effect size stool: meta-analysis, the analysis of statistical power, and the interpretation of effect sizes.

I sent *The Essential Guide* off to Cambridge University Press, and they published it.

Then… crickets.

I would like to say that the publication of my book revolutionized the world of research, but it didn't. Sales started out slow and only began to take off after a few years.

What was immediately successful, however, was a little website I put up to plug the book. Within a short time, the website received more than a million hits with traffic growing every month. The website is called www.effectsizefaq.com and it has some useful resources for researchers.

My textbook has everything you need to come to grips with effect sizes, but for some readers it may be too big a step into a strange new world. By gauging site visits, I have learned that most researchers are simply looking for answers to three questions:

(1) What is an effect size?
(2) How do I calculate the statistical power of my study?
(3) How do I draw definitive conclusions from inconclusive studies?

The book you are reading answers the first question. Two other books in the MadMethods series, *Statistical Power Trip* and *Meta-Analysis Made Easy*, answer the second and third questions respectively. (Value tip: You get three-books-in-one for a low price in the box set version.)

Why did I write these little books when I have already written a perfectly good text? Because students are poor and researchers are busy. You probably don't have six months to come to grips with these new subjects. You just want the short version.

Perhaps you have a deadline approaching or a reviewer breathing down your neck. Your attitude is, "I don't have time to read a dense text. I just wish someone could show me how to report and interpret effect sizes and quickly!"

Your wish is granted.

Paul D. Ellis

What is an effect size?

Let's begin with two definitions:

> An **effect** is the result of something. It is an outcome, a result, a reaction, a change in Y brought about by a change in X.

> An **effect size** refers to the magnitude of the outcome as it occurs, or would be found, in nature or in a population. Although effects can be observed in the artificial setting of a laboratory or a sample, effect sizes exist in the real world.

Table 1 contains a brief list of famous effects and the scientists who studied them.

Effect sizes are ubiquitous. You can find them in newspapers, college brochures, shop windows, Facebook ads, product packaging, church newsletters, blogs, tweets, TV commercials—just about anywhere.

Here are some everyday examples of effect size:

- lose 20 pounds in four weeks on the South Beach diet
- learn how to speak Swahili in six months
- make $2,300 a day working from home
- improve test performance through meditation

- fast-track your career with an MBA
- list your property with us and sell your home within a week
- read this book and improve your publication prospects

Table 1: Classic effects in science

How does this *X*...	...affect this *Y*?	Who?
gravity	celestial mechanics (and apples)	Isaac Newton (1680s)
cowpox vaccinations	smallpox immunity	Edward Jenner (1790s)
contaminated water	cholera outbreaks	John Snow (1850s)
alternating current	long distance transmission	Nikola Tesla (1880s)
semi-dwarf wheat	crop yields	Norman Borlaug (1950s)
aspirin	clotting diseases	Harvey Weiss (1960s)
bacteria	stomach ulcers	Barry Marshall (1980s)
legalized abortion	crime rates	Steven Levitt (1990s)
governance	economic development	Jeffrey Sachs (2000s)

All of these claims promise some sort of effect (a fast-tracked career, a sold home). Some even dare to promise effects of measurable size ("make $2,300 a day," "lose 20 pounds in four weeks"). No understanding of statistical significance is necessary to gauge the merits of these claims. Each is described in plain English using metrics that can be understood by just about anyone.

Every day we make decisions based on the analysis of effect sizes. We start diets because we believe they will help us to lose weight. We spend huge sums of money on education because we hope to earn higher incomes later. And we buy books on effect sizes because we expect they will help us become better researchers.

The interpretation of effect sizes is how we make sense of the world.

We will return to the issue of interpretation in Part B. But first, we need to learn how to measure or estimate effect sizes.

How to estimate an effect size

Effects exist in the real world — in populations rather than laboratories. The best way to measure an effect is to conduct a census of an entire population. But as this is often not practicable, researchers typically estimate effects by observing representative samples. Thus we can distinguish effect sizes from our sample-based estimates of those effect sizes:

- effect sizes are real, extant, *out there*
- sample-based estimates of effect sizes are shadows or approximations of the real thing

Recall the Hindu tale of the blind men and the elephant (see Figure 1). None of the men had encountered an elephant before and groping about in their blindness each drew different conclusions.

The man touching the elephant's leg concluded, "An elephant is like a tree." "No," said the man touching the ear. "An elephant is like a fan." "You're both wrong," said the man holding the trunk. "An elephant is like a snake."[1]

---

[1] John Godfrey Saxe (1872), "The blind men and the elephant."

Figure 1: The blind men and the elephant

The elephant represents the effect size. It is what it is. The blind men represent researchers groping about with their sample-based studies. Each sample provides a snapshot of the elephant but doesn't necessarily give an accurate picture of the elephant as a whole. It is only when we put all the sample-based evidence together that the elephant begins to appear.

Since researchers with limited resources are like blind men, it is unwise to look at the results of a single study and conclude, "The effect size is exactly like this" or "The effect size is exactly this big." A safer conclusion would be as follows:

> Based on my results, I estimate the effect size is equivalent to $d = 0.45$. After reviewing estimates obtained from other studies in this area, I tentatively conclude that the effect size is likely to be within the 0.42–0.58 range.

This is a far more precise and reasonable conclusion than saying:

> I found a statistically significant result so there must be some effect. Since five out of eight previous studies found the same thing, I conclude that there is some positive relationship of unknown size. Those other three studies, which returned nonsignificant results, must've been done by sloppy researchers.

An illustration may help. About twenty years ago I did a study examining the effect of a market orientation on business performance. This is a very important effect because if being customer-oriented doesn't boost performance, what's the point of going to business school?

Happily, I found that a market orientation *does* have a positive effect on business performance. (Good news, B-Schools!) The more customer- and competitor-oriented you are, the better you will perform. But how big is this effect? Based on the results of my solitary study, I estimated the effect size to be equivalent to a correlation of $r = 0.25$ (Ellis 2007).

But here's the problem. My result was based on just one sample. There must be a million companies in the world and I only studied a few hundred of them. I was in danger of being the blind man who mistook elephants for trees.

To draw a more definitive conclusion, I needed to compare my study-specific estimate with estimates obtained in other studies. I did this by pooling published and unpublished effect sizes reported by others.

Altogether, I was able to identify 58 relevant studies with a combined sample size of 14,586 firms from 28 countries. When you think how many firms there in the world, this is still a drop in the bucket, but with this massive sample I was a lot closer to seeing the elephant.

From this combined set of studies I calculated a mean effect size of $\bar{r} = .26$ and a 95 percent confidence interval of .25–.28 (Ellis 2006).[2] This told me that the estimate of the effect size observed in my individual study was within the likely range of values for the true effect size. I had seen the elephant!

But I am getting ahead of myself. You may be wondering, "What's all this talk about *d* and *r*?"

---

[2] I talk about how and why I conducted this meta-analysis—and the big mistake I made doing it—in Book 3, *Meta-Analysis Made Easy.*

Two families of effect size

Effect sizes come in many shapes and sizes. Some have familiar names like odds ratio and relative risk. Some double-up as test statistics (e.g., r, R^2), and others sound like planets from Star Trek (e.g., the Pillai-Bartlett V).

To be honest, I can't name all the effect sizes. But then, it's possible no one can. Kirk (2003) reckons there are at least 70 varieties but that number likely grows with each new statistical innovation.

Effect sizes are a bit like elements on the periodic table. There are some basic and well-known indexes at one end and some obscure and recently discovered indexes at the other.

The good news is that you don't need to know all the effect size indexes. All you really need to know is that most of them can be grouped into one of two families:

1. the d family, which includes indexes assessing the differences between groups
2. the r family, which includes measures of association

The *d* family: how different are these groups?

Are women drivers better than male drivers? Are right-handed batters more successful than lefties? Are those in the treatment group better off than those in the control group? Answers to these sorts of questions may be dichotomous (e.g., yes/no, pass/fail) or continuous (e.g., test scores) in nature.

When we compare groups on dichotomous variables, comparisons may be based on the probabilities of group members being classified into one of the two categories. Relevant effect sizes for this sort of comparison include the **odds ratio** and **relative risk**.

These two indexes are similar but different. Relative risk compares the *probability* of an outcome occurring in one group with the probability of it occurring in another, while the odds ratio compares the *odds* of an outcome occurring in one group with the odds of it occurring in another. If you know the difference between probabilities (p) and odds ($p/1 - p$), you know the difference between these two indexes.

When we compare groups on continuous variables the usual practice is to gauge the difference in the average or mean scores of each group. In theory, this is quite simple:

$$\frac{M_1 - M_2}{SD_{population}}$$

To calculate the difference between two groups we subtract the mean of one group from the mean of the other ($M_1 - M_2$) and divide the result by the standard deviation (*SD*) of the population from which the groups have been sampled. Easy peasy lemon squeezy!

The only tricky part in this calculation is figuring out the population standard deviation. Typically this number is unknown so we must rely on some approximate value instead. Since there are at least three ways to come up with that value, there are three ways to calculate the mean difference between two groups:

Cohen's *d*	Glass's Δ	Hedges' *g*
$$\frac{M_1 - M_2}{SD_{pooled}}$$	$$\frac{M_1 - M_2}{SD_{control}}$$	$$\frac{M_1 - M_2}{SD^*_{pooled}}$$

Which is best? It depends.

When comparing groups a good way to proceed is to examine the standard deviations of each group. If they are about the same we can reasonably assume they are estimating a common population standard deviation. In this case we would pool the two SDs to calculate a **Cohen's *d*.** If they are not the same we could assume that the SD of the control group is closer to the true population SD and calculate a **Glass's Δ** or delta. And if the groups are dissimilar in size we could pool the weighted SD's and calculate a **Hedges' g**.

(If you're interested, equations for fiddling around with standard deviations are found in *The Essential Guide to Effect Sizes*. If you're not interested, but you have to do it anyway, just plug your numbers into an online calculator such as the one I'll tell you about below.)

The *r* family: how strong is this relationship?

How strong are the links between smoking and cancer, Facebook use and academic performance, kissing and Covid-19? These sorts of questions lead to effect sizes of the second kind, namely, measures of association linking two or more variables. Many of these measures are variations on the **correlation coefficient** (*r*), for instance, the **rank correlation coefficient**, the **point-biserial correlation coefficient**, *R* **squared**, **eta squared**, and so forth.

If you have done any sort of stats course, you will know about *r* and its derivatives. What you may not know is that r is one of the most popular measures of effect size.

There are dozens of effect size index and you don't need to know them all. However, you should have a passing familiarity with some of the more popular metrics, and these are listed in Table 2.

Table 2: Fifteen common effect size indexes

The *d* Family	The *r* Family

Groups compared on...
(a) dichotomous outcomes
  - the risk difference (RD) in probabilities
  - the risk ratio or relative risk (RR)
  - the odds ratio (OR)
	(a) Correlation indexes
	  - the Pearson product moment correlation coefficient (r)
	  - Spearman's rho or the rank correlation coefficient (ρ or r_s)
	  - point-biserial correlation coefficient (r_{pb})
	  - the phi coefficient (φ)

(b) continuous outcomes
  - Cohen's *d*
  - Glass's Δ
    Hedges' *g*
	(b) Proportion of variance indexes
	  - the coefficient of determination (r^2)
	  - R squared, or the (uncorrected) coefficient of multiple determination (R^2)
	  - adjusted R squared ($_{adj}R^2$)
	  - Cohen's *f*
	  - eta squared or the (uncorrected) correlation ratio (η^2)

How to calculate an effect size

Often when I tell people about effect sizes, one of the first things they ask is, "What software do I need to calculate them?" That's a bit like saying, "What do I need to catch an animal?" It depends on the animal.

There is no one-size-fits-all program that will generate effect sizes for every situation, and you don't really need one. Effect size indexes in the *d* family can be calculated on the back of an envelope or in a spreadsheet. If you can subtract and divide you can calculate Glass's Δ. Admittedly, it gets a bit more complicated when you start fiddling around with the denominator, but most of the time you will be able to find an online calculator simply by googling the name of the desired index (e.g., "Cohen's *d* calculator" or "relative risk calculator").

Effect size indexes in the *r*-family are often generated automatically by statistical programs such as SPSS or STATA.[3]

---

[3] For a list of SPSS procedures that can be used to calculate 25 common effect size indexes, see Table 1.2 in *The Essential Guide to Effect Sizes* (Ellis 2010b).

Can you recommend an effect size calculator?

A few years ago I hired a programmer to build a webpage with seven of the most-used calculators all in one place. I gave her the formulas and she gave me a functional website that anyone can use. Figure 2 provides a screenshot.

Figure 2: Effect size calculators[4]

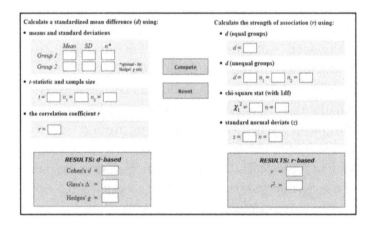

How does it work? Let's say you are comparing two groups and for each group you have the usual descriptive statistics (means and SDs). By plugging these four numbers into the boxes on the top-left of the page and then clicking the compute button in the

---

[4] Most of the resources mentioned in this book can be accessed from effectsizefaq.com/resources.

middle, you will automatically get an effect size expressed in terms of Cohen's d and Glass's Δ. And if you input the group sizes as well, you'll get a Hedges' g for good measure.

Or perhaps you want to calculate the effect size of a published study but the authors neglected to include descriptive statistics. Did they include a t-stat? Then enter that number along with the two group sizes and you'll get a d-based metric.

One neat thing about this app is that it will automatically convert your d to an r, just for fun. This means if you have multiple studies examining the same effect but reporting results in different metrics, you can convert their results to a common metric and compare them. Suddenly, without trying, you have become a meta-analyst!

Why are editors increasingly asking authors to report effect sizes?

Because the whole point of doing research is so that we may learn something about real world effects.

Until recently, the publishability of any study was largely determined by the results of statistical significance tests. Get a low p value and *voila!* Your hypothesis was supported and you had a story to tell.

But that was then and this is now.

Editors are increasingly coming to realize that p values tell us very little about the phenomena we study. True, they can signal the direction of an effect (positive, negative, or none at all). But they can't tell us how big the effect is. And if we can't say whether the effect is large or small, how can we draw meaningful conclusions? How can we interpret our result?

Let's say you're interested in the effect of sun-bathing on skin cancer. You read every study you can find on sun-bathing and skin cancer, you design a study to assess the link between sun-bathing and skin cancer, and you collect data on sun-bathing and skin cancer. But what happens next? Do you tell us how strong the relationship is? Not if you're among the 95 percent of researchers who subscribe to null hypothesis significance testing. No, you test a hypothesis no one is interested in, namely, the null hypothesis that sun-bathing has *no effect* on skin cancer. If all goes well, you reject that straw man. If the sign is in the expected direction, you'll conclude that, "Yes, there is an effect; sun-bathing has some effect on skin cancer."

And what have we learned?

Precisely nothing.

We already knew that sun bathing leads to skin cancer. (We've read the previous studies too.) What we really want to know is, how big is this effect and what does it mean? Should we change our sun bathing behavior? Should we stop sun-bathing? Your null hypothesis significance test can't answer these questions—it's not designed to. Consequently, your contribution to knowledge is close to zilch.

Editors understand this which is why they are now asking for more. Look at your data again. How big is the r (if you have one) or the d (ditto)? How do your estimates of the effect size compare with estimates obtained in other studies? Are the estimates converging on a common population effect size or are they diverging for predictable reasons? And what do your results mean for the average sun-bather?

After all, isn't this why you're doing the research in the first place—to save sun-bathers?

Which journals encourage the reporting of effect sizes?

Editors encourage effect size reporting two ways: (1) by explicitly asking authors to report effect sizes in their submission guidelines, or (2) by asking authors to interpret the substantive significance of their findings (which can only be done by examining effect sizes). Editors and editorial board members who deserve praise for promoting effect size reporting are listed in Table 3.

This may not be a particularly large list, but look at the journals on it. Some of them are among the best in their fields. They are the trend-setters. It is inevitable that this list will grow as reporting practices promulgated in the top-tier journals are adopted by others.

The journal I am submitting to says nothing about reporting effect sizes. Should I do it anyway?

Of course! How else will you interpret the substantive significance of your results without referring to your effect size estimates? (Remember, this is one of five compelling reasons mentioned at the start of this book for reporting effect sizes.)

Table 3: Editors who encourage effect size reporting

Journal	Editor
Academy of Management J.	Combs (2010), Rynes (2007)
Educational & Psychological Measurement	Thompson (1994)
J. of Applied Psychology	Campbell (1982), Murphy (1997), Zedeck (2003)
J. of Consulting & Clinical Psychology	Kendall (1997), La Greca (2005)
J. of Consumer Research	Iacobucci (2005)
J. of Counseling and Development	Thompson (2002)
J. of Educational Psychology	JEP (2003)
J. of Experimental Psychology	Melton (1962)
J. of Family Psychology	Levant (1992)
J. of Int. Business Studies	Shaver (2006)
J. of Learning Disabilities	Hresko (2000)
J. of Rehabilitation	Lustig and Strauser (2004)
Personnel Psychology	Campion (1993)
Research in the Schools	McLean and Kaufman (2000)

Researchers who focus on the results of statistical significance tests at the expense of effect sizes are under-selling their results. They are essentially throwing away hard-earned data and settling for contributions that are less than what they really have to offer.

They are like the proverbial prosecutor trying to win his case without referring to the evidence.

It is true that many journals presently do not require the reporting of effect sizes. Scan the author guidelines for some journals and you won't even find the phrase "effect size." But you can bet your house that this will change over time, and that a growing number of disciplines will follow the lead of psychology because effect size reporting is the right and smart thing to do.

It is a habit we should have adopted 40 years ago.

And although many editors may have no explicit policy on effect size reporting, you may encounter reviewers who do. I have served on seven editorial review boards and reviewed countless papers and I always insist on the reporting of effect sizes. I am utterly pedantic about it. This is not about me promoting a pet statistical technique; I simply want to see the evidence that authors have collected. So do others.

A paper that doesn't report effect sizes is like a whodunit novel without the final chapter or a riddle without a punch line. It is unfinished. By coaching authors through the review process I have helped many tease out results and contributions that were far more meaningful than what they thought they had.

Why haven't I heard about effect sizes before?

The simple answer is you are probably not a psychologist.

Methodological innovations have to come from somewhere and in the social sciences, many originate in the field of psychology. Read any top psychology journal and you may be surprised at the emphasis given to methodology and statistical innovation. Evidently, there is something about the study of psychology that appeals to statisticians. Or maybe it's the other way around.

Effect sizes may be new to you but Jacob Cohen, formerly of NYU's psychology department, was writing brilliant little papers about them 60 years ago (Cohen 1962). In the 1970s, Gene Glass and Mary Lee Smith collected effect sizes in their pioneering meta-analysis of psychotherapy treatments (Glass 1976, Smith and Glass 1977).

By the 1990s Wilkinson and the Taskforce on Statistical Inference, in their recommendations to the American Psychological Association, were arguing that the reporting and interpretation of effect sizes is "essential to good research" (1999: 599). So effect sizes have been around for some time.

In my own discipline, international business, very few researchers are in the habit of reporting and interpreting effect sizes. This may be the case with your discipline as well.

But if history has taught us anything, it's that psychology is the Silicon Valley of statistical reform. Innovations and practices developed there are often adopted later in other social science disciplines. After all, these are the guys who wrote the manual most of us follow when submitting our papers for publication. I am referring to the *Publication Manual of the American Psychological Association*, which says this:

> For the reader to appreciate the magnitude or importance of a study's findings, it is almost always necessary to include some measure of effect size in the Results Section. (APA 2010: 34)

If psychologists are big believers in effect size reporting, odds are this practice will become commonplace in other disciplines. So get in ahead of the pack and develop the habit of reporting and interpreting effect sizes.

Why wasn't I taught effect sizes in Research Methods 101?

Good question! The most likely answer is that your teacher was never taught about effect sizes and you can't teach what you haven't learned.

As I mentioned, I taught Research Methods to Ph.D. students for 15 years and for part of that time I was ignorant of effect sizes. It wasn't until I began learning about meta-analysis that I realized the estimation of effect sizes is a fundamental, if oft-ignored, goal of all research. Hopefully your teachers were better-informed than me, but odds are they weren't.

Why does my research methods textbook have no entry for "effect size"?

Because it's out of date. It's a dinosaur, a relic of a bygone age.

As a methods teacher I have accumulated a substantial library of methods books. Prior to writing *The Essential Guide to Effect Sizes*, I scanned all of these books plus dozens more in the library to see if they said *anything* about effect sizes. I discovered that close to 90 percent of textbooks said nothing at all, and the few that did mention effect sizes usually did so only in passing (e.g., with reference to meta-analysis).

My library tour sadly confirmed the perception that many textbooks are 20–30 years behind the game. On the one hand, we have the editors of prestigious journals and the presidents of academic societies calling for the reporting of effect sizes; on the other, we have methods texts and methods classes that are doing nothing in response to those calls. It was this disconnect that prompted me to write the book you are now reading.

A typical methods text will show you how a hundred different ways to assess the statistical significance of a test, but it won't show you how to interpret the substantive significance of your results. It will talk about p values but say next to nothing about effect sizes.

This will change.

As the number of journal editors insisting on effect size reporting continues to grow, the number researchers learning how to report them will also grow. Some will write books about it. My guess is that in 10–20 years' time, effect sizes will be covered in the majority of methods texts.

You read it here first.

Intermission

In Part A our focus was on reporting estimates of the effect size. One of the reasons we do this is so that we can draw conclusions about real world effects.

If the question in Part A was, "how big is it?" the question we now turn to in Part B is, "what does it mean and to whom?"

How to answer the most important question you'll ever be asked in a research presentation

"So what?"

"Why did you do this study?"

"What impact does this have for the real world?"

These questions provoke nervous smiles and evasive answers, but they are legitimate questions that deserve legitimate answers. They certainly deserve answers better than these:

"This study contributes to our understanding of XYZ." *Whoop-de-doo.*

"The results shed light on the relationship between X and Y." *Yawn. Somebody fetch me a pillow.*

"The findings show that Y is affected by X." *We probably could've guessed that without doing a study. Why not tell us how big the effect is and what it means.*

"The results provide further evidence of a link between X and Y." *After three years of careful study that's it?! You're telling us you discovered something we already knew?*

It's responses like these that give researchers a bad name.

Failing to communicate the real world significance of our work reinforces the public's perception that academics are no earthly good, that we teach because we can't do, and that we inhabit little bubbles of irrelevance.

A colleague of mine once compared researchers to medieval alchemists. "Instead of turning base metals into gold, we're turning taxpayer's money into conference papers." Sadly, there is a measure of truth behind this cynical observation.

Researchers occupy a privileged position in society. We exist at the pleasure of the taxpayer or benefactor. So when society asks the hard "so what?" questions, it behooves us to offer intelligent answers. The problem is that most of us don't know how to answer these questions in any meaningful way. We have never been taught how. We know how to collect and analyze data but the bit that comes after that remains a mystery.

How do most researchers draw conclusions from their studies?

Since most of us have not been taught to report effect sizes, it follows that most of us don't know how to interpret them. And if we're not interpreting effect sizes, what are we interpreting instead? On what basis are we drawing conclusions from our studies?

Many researchers draw conclusions by looking at the results of statistical significance tests. They follow what we might call a p-based logic of ascribing meaning. This p-based logic runs like this:

- if $p > .10$, then the test result is interpreted as providing no support for the hypothesis
- if $.05 < p < .10$, the result is interpreted as providing marginal support
- if $p < .05$, the result is interpreted as supporting the hypothesis

I have seen some studies that go even further and interpret a result of $p < .01$ or $.001$ as "strong support" or "strong confirmation" or "strong evidence" for whatever they are looking for (see Figure 3).

It's a common practice to interpret the substantive significance of a test result by looking at its statistical significance, but it's bad science.

Figure 3: The relationship between *p*-values and researcher happiness

Statistical significance tests have their uses — they are useful for managing the risk of mistaking random sampling variation for genuine effects — but we cannot use them to draw substantive conclusions about the effects we are studying. Why not? A story will help explain...

What is the difference between and effect size and a *p* value?

Two groups of sports fans argued over who knew more about wrestling. Rednecks argued that slack-jawed yokels "don't know the first thang 'bout rassling," while the SJY's replied that "yer average redneck cain't tell diff'rence 'tween the dub-dub-F and the dub-dub-E."

The bickering continued until both groups decided to settle the matter with a quiz about wrestling trivia. To keep things fair and above board, each group recruited an independent researcher to administer the test.

Since neither group trusted the other, the same test was done twice, one after the other. In each test, rednecks and SJYs were asked a set of questions about wrestling. To no one's surprise, the results of both studies, in terms of test scores and standard deviations, turned out to be exactly the same (see Table 4).

Although both studies found that rednecks scored higher than SJYs, the results from Study 2 were not statistically significant (i.e., $p > .05$). This led the author of Study 2 to conclude that there was no statistical difference between the groups in terms of their knowledge of wrestling trivia.

However, the author of Study 1 came to a different conclusion. She noted that the 25–point difference in mean test scores was substantial in size being just less than one standard deviation. This author concluded that rednecks are substantially more knowledgeable than SJYs when it comes to wrestling trivia.

Table 4: Test scores for knowledge of wrestling trivia

	Mean	SD	N	t	p	Cohen's d
Study 1						
Rednecks	75	30	25	1.84	< .05	0.83
SJYs	50	30	25			
Study 2						
Rednecks	75	30	20	1.65	> .05	0.83
SJYs	50	30	20			

The author of Study 1 said there was a big difference between the groups, while the author of Study 2 said there was no difference. How could two studies with identical methods relying on identical samples to estimate identical effect sizes lead to such different conclusions?

The answer has to do with the misuse of statistical significance testing. When interpreting the results of their study, the author of Study 2 ignored the estimate of the effect size and focused on the p value. He incorrectly interpreted a statistically nonsignificant result as indicating no effect. However, a nonsignificant result is more accurately interpreted as an *inconclusive* result. There might be no effect, or there might be an effect but the study lacked the statistical power to detect it. In this case we have good reason to lean towards the latter conclusion.

Why so?

Take another look in the numbers in Table 4 paying particular attention to the descriptive stats. A 25 point difference between the group means seems big, but in truth it's meaningless unless we know something about the standard deviation or the spread of the results. The d (0.83) in the far right column tells us that the difference between the groups is equivalent to five-sixths of a standard deviation. That is a big difference in anyone's language. It tells us that rednecks are considerably smarter than SJYs.

The author of Study 1 saw this whopper of a difference but the author of Study 2 missed it. How?

He was distracted by his p value.

This begs the question, if the effect was so big, how come the statistical test didn't bear fruit in Study 2?

And how come it did in Study 1? Why did these identical studies generate different p values?

The reason is that after the first study, ten participants thought it was stupid to take the same test again so they went home. Hence the conclusions for Study 2 were drawn from a smaller pooled sample (40 people instead of 50) and the consequent drain on statistical power meant that a genuine effect went undetected.

This leads us to one of the most important questions in this book…

Why can't we draw substantive conclusions from p values?

Because p values are affected by several factors, only one of which is the size of the underlying effect. Here's an equation to illustrate this point:

statistical significance = effect size x sample size

Statistical significance is inversely proportional to the p value of a test result. A high p means the result is not statistically significant and vice versa. What the equation above tells us is that, other things being equal, the bigger the effect the smaller the p. In other words, the bigger the thing you are trying to find, the easier it is to find it—the more likely your results will be statistically significant. So a small p could indicate a large effect size, but not necessarily.

Now look at the other side of that equation. All things being equal, the bigger the sample the smaller the p. In other words, the wider your net, the more likely you'll catch something, even if the thing you're fishing for is tiny. Conversely, the smaller the sample the bigger the p. As samples shrink it becomes harder to achieve statistical significance even when large effects are being observed.

In the wrestling example, the effect size was identical in both studies but the sample size was smaller for study 2. (Ten people went home, remember?) As N went down, p went up. It had to—sample size and statistical significance are directly related. This is why the test results differed between the studies.

I cover these issues in my MadMethods book *Statistical Power Trip*. All you need to know here is that you should never judge the substantive significance of a result by looking at a p value. P values are confounded indexes. They are affected by several variables only one of which is the effect size.

To draw any sort of substantive conclusion from a result, you need to look directly at the estimate of the effect size. This could be a d-equivalent variable if you are comparing groups, or some variation of r if you are examining the strength of association. But unless you know what *It* is and how big *It* is, then you won't be able to say anything meaningful about *It*.

Capiche?

"I got a significant result"—what's wrong with this statement?

In a typical methods class, students are taught to assess the statistical significance of their results. This is a useful skill but it can lead to meaningless claims like the one above. My students quickly learned never to say things like that.

"Professor, I got a significant result!"

"Grrrrrr!"

What's the problem? The problem is the word significant requires qualification. What type of significance are we talking about? Because there is more than one:

- statistical significance = the result exceeds certain statistical criteria
- practical or substantive significance = the result is meaningful in the real world

Think of it this way: Only researchers and statisticians understand the first kind of significance, while the second kind makes sense to real people like plumbers, painters, and publicans. Since we are attempting to do research that matters, we need to be as familiar with the latter as the former.

Since there are at two kinds of significance, there are four possible outcomes for any research result. A result can be statistically significant and practically meaningless, vice versa, neither, or both. To say, "I got a significant result," begs the question, "What sort of significance are we talking about?"

Usually, it's the wrong sort.

Don't get me wrong, statistical significance is nice to have. But at the end of the day what really matters is substantive significance. To see how well you understand this, consider the following research scenario, which is adapted from Kirk (1996):

> You are testing a new drug which you hope will improve the IQ of Alzheimer's patients. You administer the drug to a test group and a placebo to a control group. After some time you test both groups and find...

Outcome 1   The treatment group now has an average IQ 13 points higher than the control group — an appreciable difference. However, the p value is high (.14) making the result statistically nonsignificant.

Outcome 2 The difference between the groups is small, just 2 IQ points, but the p value is low (0.04) making the result statistically significant.

Which outcome do you prefer? Review the two outcomes again and take a moment to decide which one you would rather see.

Have you made your choice? Okay. This is not a trick question. Outcome 1 is clearly better. A thirteen point improvement is better than a two point improvement. But if you hesitated before choosing this outcome, or worse, you chose Outcome 2, then that should tell you something.

Perhaps you dismissed the results of Outcome 1 as a fluke. After all, the results are statistically nonsignificant. If so, then you risk discarding a potentially brilliant cure.

Or perhaps you got excited about the statistically significant result of Outcome 2. If so, you risk directing future research down a dead end. You could spend the next five to ten years of your career invested in a drug that probably doesn't work.

Look again at the effect sizes (the change in IQ) and make a judgment without regard for the p value. Wouldn't you agree that a thirteen point gain is a bigger and intrinsically more interesting result than a two point gain? Outcome 2 gave us a statistically significant result, but Outcome 1 gave us a result of substantive significance.

What would I do with these two outcomes? In the case of Outcome 1, I would be encouraged to do a bigger study. We may be on to a winner and chances are the low p value is the result of an underpowered research design. In the case of Outcome 2, I would be tempted to abandon the drug and move on to other things. It seems to be a dud.

Anyway, we were talking about the different meanings of significance.

In research it is possible, and unfortunately quite common, for a result to be statistically significant yet trivial. It is also possible for a result to be statistically nonsignificant yet meaningful.

However, researchers rarely distinguish between these two types of significance. What usually happens is that results which are found to be statistically significant are interpreted as if they were practically meaningful. This happens when a researcher interprets a statistically significant result as "significant" or "highly significant."

Do researchers really get confused about this significance stuff?

I surveyed six years' worth of research in a leading business journal to assess the extent to which researchers in my field are in the habit of reporting and interpreting effect sizes. My survey covered 204 independent studies reported in 189 separate articles (see Ellis 2010a).

In many of the studies I read, effect sizes were reported unintentionally. This occurred whenever authors reported test statistics that happen to double as effect size indicators (e.g., r, R^2, η^2). However, very few studies mentioned effect sizes explicitly. Consequently, it was no great surprise to find authors drawing conclusions that, frankly, were meaningless.

Some authors mentioned that their models "performed well." *Performed well with respect to what?* Others observed that their combination of predictors generated R^2s (or an increase in R^2s) that were "respectable" or "remarkable." *Respectable or remarkable in comparison with what?* Without a frame of reference, claims like these are meaningless.

Here are some other examples of meaningless conclusions that I came across:

- In one study statistical significance tests revealed that X had a positive influence on Y, "providing strong confirmation of (the effect)." *They provided no such thing. Statistical significance is affected by multiple factors, only one of which is the effect size.*

- "Test results provide strong evidence that Y ($p <$ 0.01) is a function of X." *I don't doubt that there is evidence of a link in your study but that low p reveals nothing about the strength of such a link. Chances are you just had a really large sample.*

- "Overall the empirical model performs well: it is highly significant, and records a pseudo-R^2 of 0.37, which is respectable for logit models." *This would be funny if it wasn't so cringeworthy. It's like there's this country club for respectable logit models. Models which achieve lower R-squareds aren't welcome. They can go hang out in a B-grade journal with the other riff-raff.*

- One author observed a "remarkable jump" in R^2. *Goody! Maybe they'll let him into that exclusive club for respectable logits.*

- "All the coefficients have the hypothesized sign and are significant." *[Insert anguished sounds of frustration and hair-pulling here.] I am happy for you that the signs are as expected; I am not happy that you are blurring the lines between substantive and statistical significance. Take care, you're confusing the children! Ph.D. students are reading this.*

Equally meaningless was the claim that a test statistic was bigger or more impressive than a result obtained in an earlier study. If separate studies are estimating the same population effect then results should be celebrated for converging, rather than diverging. If they are estimating different effects then there is little to be gained by comparing them.

Reading these studies, it soon became clear that the majority of international business researchers do not report nor interpret their estimates of effect size. One notable exception was Baggs and Brander's (2006, p.207) attempt to convey in plain English the "economic significance" of the effects of trade liberalization in Canada:

> The effect of a large import tariff reduction reduces profit by $146,000 for an average firm. At this rate, many firms protected by initially large tariffs would have profits reduced to zero over the phase-in period.

This is a useful conclusion for it conveys information about the size of an effect in language that is meaningful to non-specialists and uncomplicated by subsidiary issues of statistical significance. Regrettably, conclusions as clear as this were hard to find.

My survey results are not unusual. The common finding of similar surveys in other disciplines is that most authors make no attempt to interpret the practical or real world significance of their research results (see, for example, Andersen *et al.*, 2007; Kieffer *et al.*, 2001; McCloskey and Ziliak 1996).

Even scholars publishing in top-tier journals routinely confuse statistical with practical significance. In their review of 137 papers published in the *American Economic Review*, Ziliak and McCloskey (2004) found that 82 percent of authors mistook statistical significance for economic significance.

Eighty-two percent!

Cohen (1994: 1001) drew a similar conclusion after observing his colleagues' habits in the field of psychology.

> All psychologists know that *statistically significant* does not mean plain English significant, but if one reads the literature, one often discovers a finding reported in the Results section studded with asterisks implicitly becomes in the Discussion section highly significant, or very highly significant, important, big!

I've got an effect size — now what?

Interpret it. Use your own informed judgment to tell us what it means.

In the Alzheimer's example, I got excited about the prospect of a thirteen point gain in IQ. But since I have no experience working with Alzheimer's patients I don't really know how meaningful a thirteen point gain is. So let me ask you what you think.

Imagine that someone you care about is suffering from advanced Alzheimer's. If a thirteen point gain in IQ meant they could now remember your name and face, would you judge that to be a "significant" improvement? You probably would.

Okay, what about a gain that was only half as big, say, six IQ points? Still significant? It's harder to say but only you can make this judgment. There's no book you can look up to decide whether a six point improvement is meaningful. It's meaningful if you say it is; it's not if you say it isn't.

Here's the point: effects mean different things to different people. What is a big deal to you may not be a big deal to me and vice versa. The interpretation of effect sizes inevitably involves a value judgment and this makes researchers uncomfortable. We prefer the cold distance of objectivity to the warm-fuzzies of subjective interpretation. We would rather be Mr. Spock than Captain Kirk.

But if you don't interpret your own findings, who will?

> No one is in a better position than the research-er who collected and analyzed the data to de-cide whether the effects are trivial or not. It is a curious anomaly that researchers are trusted to make a variety of complex decisions in the design and execution of an experiment, but in the name of objectivity they are not expected to nor even encouraged to decide whether the effects are practically significant. (Kirk 2001:214)

Failing to interpret your study's findings is like quit-ting a marathon a quarter mile short of the finish line. You've done all the work—you've designed and executed a study—now tell us what you found and what it means.

As we have seen, the wrong way to do this is to look at p values. The right way is to look at the effect size. Is it big or small? In comparison with what? Is it big enough to be meaningful? How does it compare with what others have found?

How do I interpret my results?

Imagine your doctor tells you this:

> Research shows that people with your body-mass index and sedentary lifestyle score on average two points lower on a cardiac risk assessment test in comparison with active people with a healthy body weight.

Would these words prompt you to make drastic changes to your lifestyle? Probably not. Not because the effect is trivial but because you have no way of interpreting its meaning. What does "two points lower" mean? Is two points a big deal? Should you be worried? Being unfamiliar with the scale, you are unable to draw any conclusion.

Now imagine your doctor says this instead:

> Research shows that people with your body-mass index and sedentary lifestyle are four times as likely to suffer a serious heart attack within 10 years in comparison with active people with a normal body weight.

Now the doctor has your full attention. This time you're sitting on the edge of your seat gripped with a resolve to lose weight and start exercising again. Hearing about the research in terms which are familiar to you, you are better able to extract their meaning and draw conclusions.

When it comes to interpreting effects, context matters. Effect sizes are meaningless unless they can be contextualized against some frame of reference, such as a well-known scale or prior findings.

Can you give us an example of how to interpret an effect size?

Earlier I mentioned how I found a relationship between market orientation and business performance equivalent to $r = 0.25$. That's the effect size, but what does it mean? What is the practical significance of this result? How do we interpret it?

A statistician would be tempted to express this result in terms of the proportion of shared variance. In other words, they'll square it (.25 x .25) and conclude that 6¼ percent of the total variance is shared between the two variables. Even if you don't know what that means, it sounds small—just 6¼ percent. That sounds like market orientation does not have much of an effect on performance at all.

That's one conclusion; here's another.

Business performance is affected by a thousand different factors. Some factors, like product design, branding, etc., are controllable, while many other factors, like the cost of materials, the exchange rate, the weather, pandemics, etc., are uncontrollable. It is rare for any single factor to account for a substantial proportion of business performance—there are just too many variables at play. So to find a single factor, market orientation, that accounts for 6¼ percent is noteworthy.

The world of business is complex. The average size of any effect in business is very low, just $r = 0.06$ (Ellis 2010a). Finding an effect of size $r = 0.25$ is like finding a whale in a fish tank. It stands out.

When it comes to interpreting results, context matters. In absolute terms, market orientation has a smallish effect on performance. But compared to every other factor, it has a relatively big effect. Knowing and responding to customers better than rivals is the gas pedal of business. Learning how to do this well is one thing managers and business owners can do to maximize their performance.

Allow me to recap in case you missed my point. I *reported* a smallish effect size then I *interpreted* it by comparing it with other factors affecting performance. Most effects in business are tiny; my one was bigger than tiny so it stands out. And because performance affects the life and death of any business, any effect that is bigger than the rest is likely to matter a great deal. See? By contextualizing my finding against other business effects, I gave meaning to my result.

In the Baggs and Brander (2006) study, the authors said that the effect of a large tariff reduction would be to reduce profit by $146,000 for an average firm. By conveying the effect size in terms of dollars and cents, instead of, say, p values, model fits, or changes in R^2s, these authors deliver a startlingly clear interpretation of the effect size. If you are the manager of an average firm, you will be left with an excellent idea of what the proposed tariff reduction means for your business.

It's small, but is it important?

Effect sizes are like animals; the big ones are few in number (like elephants) while the little ones are abundant (like ants). Often your research will reveal an effect which is tiny. That doesn't mean it is trivial. Some of the most interesting effects in science are small.

In the right context, small effects may be big enough to be meaningful. Presidential elections are sometimes decided on the smallest of margins. Gold medals and Olympic glory go to those who win by hundredths of a second. Just as small sparks start big fires, small effects are substantively significant when they trigger large outcomes.

Small effects can also be important if they accumulate into larger effects, such as lives saved. Consider a drug that reduces the risk of heart attacks by four percent for at-risk people. That doesn't sound like a big effect but in a large country such as the United States, this figure translates into 6,500 saved lives every year. (The drug is propranolol if you're wondering (Kolata 1981).)

Smoking gives us another example of the cumulative significance of small effects. Smokers like to argue

77

that a single cigarette does little damage. "Just one can't hurt." In fact, scientists have calculated that a smoked cigarette will shorten your life by about eleven minutes. If you are regular smoker, those minutes add up fast. Smoke a daily packet of 20 cigarettes and you will shorten your life by a day for every week that you smoke (BBC 1999). Ouch!

The accumulation of small effects into big outcomes is often seen in sports. Consider "Abelson's Paradox" which describes how trivial effects can accumulate into meaningful effects over time. It is based on research Abelson (1985) did into the effects of batting skill on individual batting performance in baseball. Abelson found that batting skill has a pitifully small on individual performance. Nevertheless, skilled batters win games because they bat more than once per game and the miniscule effects of skill cumulate.

The challenge of interpretation

We have seen that the importance of an effect is determined by its context. If you can show what the effect means in plain language, you can speak directly to its meaning. But what if you can't?

Many phenomena in the social sciences can only be observed indirectly. For instance, to assess self-esteem, trust, or satisfaction levels, you might administer a questionnaire consisting of five- or seven-point scales. You know the drill. Respondents circle numbers that best describe their response where one means "strong disagree" and seven means "strong agree." It's simple to administer, but what do you do with the results? How do you translate circled numbers or mean values into meaningful metrics?

Arbitrary scales are useful for gauging effect sizes but they make interpretation problematic. You may find that "the treated group scored 3.5 points higher on average than the untreated group," but what does that mean to the person in the street? Did the treatment work? Do the benefits outweigh the costs?

In many cases, there will be no easy answers to these sorts of questions. But if you are unable to ground your arbitrary scale against a meaningful frame of reference, you may have no way of drawing a meaningful conclusion.

Fear not. All is not lost. Jacob Cohen has come to the rescue...

Cohen's effect size thresholds

As a last resort, one way to interpret a result is to refer to conventions governing effect size. The best known of these are the thresholds proposed by Cohen (1988) in his authoritative *Statistical Power Analysis for the Behavioral Sciences*. Table 5 summarizes Cohen's criteria for five effect sizes.

TABLE 5: Cohen's effect size benchmarks

Effect size	Effect size classes		
	Small	Medium	Large
d, Δ, g	.20	.50	.80
r	.10	.30	.50
r^2	.01	.09	.25

Source: Cohen (1988)

How does it work? Say you are comparing groups and you find the difference between the groups is equivalent to $d = 0.26$. According to Cohen's logic, this would qualify as a small effect, meaning, it exceeds the 0.2 cut-off for effects of this type. In our earlier example of wrestling knowledge, the difference between rednecks and SJYs was equivalent to $d = 0.83$. According to Cohen's metric, this would qualify as a large effect as it exceeds the 0.8 cut-off for d-based metrics.

The appeal of Cohen's effect size criteria is they are convenient. You just plug in your effect size and get a ready-made interpretation.

How did Cohen come up with these thresholds?

I'm glad you asked, because there's an interesting story behind them.

In deciding the thresholds for the different effect sizes, Cohen began by defining a medium effect as one "visible to the naked eye of the careful observer" (Cohen 1992: 156). His example? The difference in height between 14 and 18 year old girls, which is about one inch (Cohen 1988: 26).

Having defined a medium-sized effect, it was a straightforward matter to define small and large effects. Cohen defined a small effect as equivalent to the height difference between 15 and 16 year old girls, which is about half an inch. A large effect was defined as one that is as far above a medium effect as a small one is below it. In this case, a large effect is equivalent to the height difference between 13 and 18 year old girls, which is just over an inch and a half.

Why did Cohen decide to look at teenage girls when deciding on these metrics? I have no idea. It's a mystery. But at least his method sounds more fun than the one adopted by Karl Pearson.

Pearson (1905) devised effect size thresholds for the correlation metric r by considering the relationship between a man's left and right thigh bones (highly correlated); the relationship between the height of fathers and their sons (considerably correlated); and the relationship between a woman's height and her pulling strength (low correlation)!

Why should we hesitate to use Cohen's thresholds?

Cohen's effect size thresholds are not without controversy. Noted scholars such as Gene Glass have argued that the classification of effects into t-shirt sizes of small, medium and large hinders real interpretation (Glass *et al.*, 1981). This is a valid point.

Earlier I mocked the convention of drawing conclusions from different p values. We might just as easily mock the convention of drawing conclusions from Cohen's thresholds. I agree with Shaver (1993: 303) who said, "Substituting sanctified effect size conventions for the sanctified .05 level of statistical significance is not progress."

To be fair, Cohen knew this when he published his thresholds. He said his conventions were devised "with much diffidence, qualifications, and invitations not to employ them if possible" (1988: 532).

The proper way to view Cohen's thresholds is as an interpretation tool of last resort. You might use them when you have no other basis for drawing meaning from your results. The fact that they are used at all—given that they have no raison d'être beyond Cohen's study of teenage girls—speaks volumes about the inherent difficulties of assessing the substantive significance of our results. Interpretation is essential but often difficult.

The good news is this issue is attracting attention from a growing number of scholars. In recent years a number of helpful guidelines have emerged to assist authors with the interpretation challenge. If you are interested, check out the work by Blanton and Jaccard (2006), Cumming and Finch (2005), Hoetker (2007), and Shaver (2008).

We'll finish this book with something fun.

The delightfully whimsical yet sort of serious Result Whacker

A few years ago I was given some grant money to develop the effect size calculators I mentioned in Part A. When I was done I had some money left over, which is criminal when dealing with bureaucratic largesse. Rather than admit my budgeting weaknesses, I gave the left-over money to a programmer with instructions to develop something called the Result Whacker (see Figure 4).

The Result Whacker is a bit of fun that serves a serious purpose. The fun part is plugging your effect size (either a d- or r-equivalent) into the relevant box, then pressing "Whack." If you have entered a large effect size, say $d = 2$ or $r = 1$, the puck flies up the tower and hits the bell. Alternatively, if your effect size is pitifully small, the puck barely moves. It's hilarious.

Well, it is if you're caffeinated to the gills after crunching numbers for ten hours straight.

Figure 4: The Result Whacker[5]

The Result Whacker is fun, but it serves an educational purpose. First, the labels on the right side of the Result Whacker correspond to Cohen's effect size conventions. If you enter $d = 0.2$, the puck will just make it to "small." But if you enter 0.1999999, the puck won't cross the threshold. Add as many 9s as you like, it's not going to get there.

So one purpose of the Whacker is to let people know that, rightly or wrongly, there are conventions out there which may be used for interpreting effects of different size.

---

[5] Source: bit.ly/RO9wj4

The second purpose of the Whacker is to make you think. After playing with the Whacker for a few minutes you begin to wonder, "Isn't this all a bit silly? Can't we do better than mindlessly plugging in numbers and whacking out a ready-made interpretation? Aren't we better than this?"

Hopefully we are.

In this regard the Result Whacker is a conversation starter, a stimulus to real interpretation.

I suppose the Result Whacker should come with a health warning. Use it without thinking and you are in just as much danger of mindless interpretation as those who draw substantive conclusions from the results of statistical significance tests.

The main takeaway from this book

In this book we have learned that most researchers fail to distinguish between the statistical- and substantive significance of their results. Consequently, most are unable to provide meaningful responses to the "so what?" question. In response, we have looked at different ways for extracting meaning from our results. We have also identified some of the pioneering journals that are now insisting on effect size reporting, and we have learned how to calculate effect sizes in a variety of metrics. If I was to distill the most important lesson of this book, it would be this: Report and interpret effect size estimates.

I said at the start that this was a book for hammer-whackers, but really there's only so much you can learn from whacking things. Real researchers *think*. They ponder and ruminate and deliberate. They entertain alternative plausible explanations and they extrapolate meaning by fitting their effect size estimates into meaningful contexts. Finally, they convey the import of their results in language that anyone can understand.

These are exciting times for researchers who believe their work can and should be of value to society. By conducting research that matters and presenting results that make sense, good researchers can change the world.

Author's note

If you enjoyed *Effect Size Matters*, would you mind posting a short customer review on Amazon? Doing so will help others find this book.

Thank you!

Appendix: Ten great quotes from dead researchers

"Research is the process of going up alleys to see if they are blind."
> — Marston Bates (1906–1974), American zoologist and author of books on ecology

"Somewhere, something incredible is waiting to be known."
> — Carl Sagan (1934–1996), American astronomer and science communicator

"Research is formalized curiosity. It is poking and prying with a purpose."
> — Zora Neale Hurston (1891–1960), American anthropologist and folklorist

"Basic research is when I am doing what I don't know what I am doing."
> — Werner von Braun (1912–1977), German scientist and designer of the Saturn V launch vehicle

"If we knew what we were doing it wouldn't be research."
> — Albert Einstein (1879–1955), the father of modern physics

"Research is to see what everybody else has seen, and to think what nobody else has thought"
— Albert Szent-Györgyi (1893–1986), Hungarian biochemist who discovered vitamin C

"By seeking and blundering we learn."
— Johann Wolfgang von Goethe (1749–1832), German science philosopher and rock collector

"What is research, but a blind date with knowledge?"
— William J. Henry (1774–1836) British chemist who formulated Henry's Law

"Research serves to make building stones out of stumbling blocks."
— Arthur D. Little (1863–1935), American chemist who discovered acetate

"Study hard what interests you the most in the most undisciplined, irreverent and original manner possible."
— Richard Feynman (1918–1988), American theoretical physicist who helped develop the atom bomb

References

Abelson, R.P. (1985), "A variance explanation paradox: When a little is a lot," *Psychological Bulletin*, 97(1): 129–133.

Andersen, M.B., P. McCullagh, and G.J. Wilson (2007), "But what do the numbers really tell us? Arbitrary metrics and effect size reporting in sport psychology research," *Journal of Sport and Exercise Psychology*, 29(5): 664–672.

APA (2010), *Publication Manual of the American Psychological Association, 6th Edition*. Washington DC: American Psychological Association.

Baggs, J. and J.A. Brander (2006), "Trade liberalization, profitability, and financial leverage," *Journal of International Business Studies*. 37(2): 196–211.

BBC (1999), "Cigarettes cut life by 11 minutes," *BBC News*, website: http://news.bbc.co.uk/2/hi/health/583722.stm

Blanton, H. and J. Jaccard (2006), "Arbitrary metrics in psychology," *American Psychologist*, 61(1): 27–41.

Campbell, J.P. (1982), "Editorial: Some remarks from the outgoing editor," *Journal of Applied Psychology*, 67(6): 691–700.

Campion, M.A. (1993), "Article review checklist: A criterion checklist for reviewing research articles in applied psychology," *Personnel Psychology*, 46(3): 705–718.

Cohen, J. (1962), "The statistical power of abnormal-social psychological research: A review," *Journal of Abnormal and Social Psychology,* 65(3): 145–153.

Cohen, J. (1988), *Statistical Power for the Behavioral Analysis, 2nd Edition.* Hillsdale: Lawrence Erlbaum.

Cohen, J. (1992), "A power primer," *Psychological Bulletin,* 112(1): 155–159.

Cohen, J. (1994), "The earth is round ($p<.05$)," *American Psychologist,* 49(12), 997–1003.

Combs, J.G. (2010), "Big samples and small effects: Let's not trade relevance and rigor for power," *Academy of Management Journal.* 53(1): 9–13.

Cumming, G. and S. Finch (2005), "Inference by eye: Confidence intervals and how to read pictures of data," *American Psychologist,* 60(2): 170–180.

Ellis, P.D. (2006), "Market orientation and performance: A meta-analysis and cross-national comparisons," *Journal of Management Studies,* 43(5): 1089–1107.

Ellis, P.D. (2007), "Distance, dependence and diversity of markets: Effects on market orientation," *Journal of International Business Studies,* 38(3): 374–386.

Ellis, P.D., (2010a) "Effect sizes and the interpretation of research results in international business," *Journal of International Business Studies,* 41(9): 1581–1588.

Ellis, P.D. (2010b), *The Essential Guide to Effect Sizes: An Introduction to Statistical Power, Meta-Analysis and the Interpretation of Research Results.* Cambridge University Press.

Glass, G. (1976), "Primary, secondary, and meta-analysis of research," *Educational Researcher* 5: 3–8.

Glass, G.V., B. McGaw, and M.L. Smith (1981), *Meta-Analysis in Social Research.* Sage: Beverly Hills.

Hoetker, G. (2007), The use of logit and probit models in strategic management research: Critical issues, *Strategic Management Journal,* 28: 331–343.

Hresko, W. (2000), "Editorial policy," *Journal of Learning Disabilities,* 33, 214–215.

Hunt, M. (1997), *How Science Takes Stock: The Story of Meta-Analysis.* New York: Russell Sage Foundation.

Iacobucci, D. (2005), "From the editor," *Journal of Consumer Research,* 32(1): 1–6.

JEP (2003), "Instructions to authors," *Journal of Educational Psychology,* 95(1): 201.

Kendall, P.C. (1997), "Editorial," *Journal of Consulting and Clinical Psychology,* 65(1): 3–5.

Kieffer, K.M., R.J. Reese, and B. Thompson (2001), "Statistical techniques employed in AERJ and JCP articles from 1988 to 1997: A methodological review," *Journal of Experimental Education,* 69(3): 280–309.

Kirk, R.E. (1996), "Practical significance: A concept whose time has come," *Educational and Psychological Measurement,* 56(5): 746–759.

Kirk, R.E. (2001), "Promoting good statistical practices: Some suggestions," *Educational and Psychological Measurement,* 61(2): 213–218.

Kirk, R.E. (2003), "The importance of effect magnitude," in S.F. Davis (editor), *Handbook of Research*

Methods in Experimental Psychology, Oxford, UK: Blackwell, 83–105.

Kolata, G.B. (1981), "Drug found to help heart attack survivors," *Science*, 214(13): 774–775.

La Greca, A.M. (2005), "Editorial," *Journal of Consulting and Clinical Psychology*, 73(1): 3–5.

Levant, R.F. (1992), "Editorial," *Journal of Family Psychology*, 6(1): 3–9.

Lustig, D. and D. Strauser (2004), "Editor's comment: Effect size and rehabilitation research," *Journal of Rehabilitation* 70(4): 3–5.

McCloskey, D.N. and S.T. Ziliak (1996), "The standard error of regressions," *Journal of Economic Literature*, 34(March): 97–114.

Melton, A. (1962), "Editorial," *Journal of Experimental Psychology*, 64(6): 553–557.

McLean, J.E. and A.S. Kaufman (2000), "Editorial: Statistical significance testing and Research in the Schools," *Research in the Schools*, 7(2).

Murphy, K.R. (1997), "Editorial," *Journal of Applied Psychology*, 82(1):3–5.

Pearson, K. (1905), "Report on certain enteric fever inoculation statistics," *British Medical Journal*, 2(2288): 1243–1246.

Rynes, S.L. (2007), "Editors afterword: Let's create a tipping point—what academics and practitioners can do, alone and together," *Academy of Management Journal*, 50(5): 1046–1054.

Shaver, J.M. (2006), "Interpreting empirical findings," *Journal of International Business Studies*, 37(4): 451–452.

Shaver, J.M. (2008), "Organizational significance," *Strategic Organization*, 6(2): 185–193.

Shaver, J.P. (1993), "What statistical significance testing is, and what it is not," *Journal of Experimental Education*, 61(4): 293–316.

Smith, M.L. and G.V. Glass (1977), "Meta-analysis of psychotherapy outcome studies," *American Psychologist*, 32(9): 752–760

Thompson, B. (1994), "Guidelines for authors," *Educational and Psychological Measurement*, 54, 837–847.

Thompson, B. (2002), "'Statistical,' 'practical,' and 'clinical': How many kinds of significance do counselors need to consider?" *Journal of Counseling and Development*, 80(1): 64–71.

Wilkinson, L. and the Taskforce on Statistical Inference (1999), "Statistical methods in psychology journals: Guidelines and expectations," *American Psychologist*, 54(8): 594–604.

Zedeck, S. (2003), "Editorial," *Journal of Applied Psychology*. 88(1): 3–5.

Ziliak, S.T. and D.N. McCloskey (2004), "Size matters: The standard error of regressions in the American Economic Review," *Journal of Socio-Economics*, 33(5): 527–546.

STATISTICAL POWER TRIP

How the Analysis of Statistical Power will
Help you Win Grants, Get Published, and have
a Successful Research Career!

PAUL D. ELLIS

Statistical Power Trip:
How the Analysis of Statistical Power will help you Win Grants, Get
Published, and Have a Successful Research Career!

Copyright © 2020 by Paul D. Ellis, 978-1-927230-57-2

Published by MadMethods, an imprint of KingsPress.org,
PO Box 66145, Beach Haven, Auckland 0749, New Zealand.

To get this title in other formats and to find other titles in the
MadMethods series, visit www.MadMethods.co

Version: 1.2 (September 2020)

Dedication: For my teachers.

"When I stumbled on power analysis… it was as if I had died and gone to heaven."

— Jacob Cohen (1990: 1308)

Why do I need this book?

Some researchers analyze words, others analyze numbers. This book is for the number-crunchers. Specifically, it is for anyone who relies on statistical inference to draw conclusions about real world effects.

But don't panic—this is not a statistics book, at least not in the usual sense. In this book you won't learn how to run a *t* test or do a logit regression or any of that stuff. What you will learn is how to ensure that whatever test you run has sufficient power to do what it is supposed to do.

Five reasons to read this book

There are at least five compelling reasons why researchers should be concerned about the statistical power of their studies:

1. Running a power analysis prevents you from engaging in research that is destined to fail. Many of the effects we study are small, yet surveys regularly show that most studies lack the power to

detect such effects. Insufficient statistical power leads to multiple problems such as wasted resources and the misdirection of future research. This book will teach you how to run a simple power analysis that will protect you from engaging in studies that are fatally under-powered or wastefully over-powered.

2. Running a power analysis improves your funding prospects. Cognizant of the dangers of insufficient power, funding agencies are increasingly asking researchers to submit the results of power analyses along with their research proposals. They want to know, "Does the proposed study have the power needed to detect the effect of interest?" Researchers who comply with these requests are setting themselves up for success, both in terms of attracting research funding and doing meaningful research.

3. Running a power analysis improves your publication prospects. Following recommendations made by the APA, editors and journal reviewers are increasingly asking authors to report on the statistical power of their studies. They want to see evidence that the study had sufficient power to detect effects of interest. Authors who provide

such evidence (e.g., the results of a power analysis) are more likely to have their papers published than those who don't.

4. Learning about statistical power will liberate you from potentially damaging allegiance to the $p < .05$ standard of statistical significance by getting you to articulate your expectations regarding the relative threat of Type I and Type II errors. It will also prompt you to evaluate results in terms of the evidence and protect you from assigning substantive significance to results that are merely statistically significant.

5. Learning about statistical power will help you avoid Type II errors. In a culture that is obsessed with the minimization of Type I errors, Type II errors have become endemic. This book will show you five ways to minimize the threat of these errors.

As we will see, the analysis of statistical power is neither difficult nor time-consuming, yet the payoffs are considerable.

A good power analysis offers enormous bang for your buck.

Who wrote this book?

I began my research career as a qualitative researcher (think case studies), but I soon succumbed to the dark side and became a number-cruncher. I have conducted countless studies in several countries using a variety of methods and statistical programs. I have won awards for research and been successful in winning numerous research grants. I have had numerous papers published in top tier journals and served on several editorial review boards.

You might consider me a successful researcher, but the truth is more complicated. I haven't told you about my many failures—projects that went nowhere, data that revealed nothing, and analyses that were flat-out wrong. One thing that long troubled me was the question that hung over every new project. *Would this study bear fruit?* Despite the toolbox of skills that I had acquired, I was never 100 percent certain that my research investments would pay off, and this bothered me.

Do you know what it's like to spend three to four years on a project only to find nothing particularly interesting? Have you ever had to bin a project because there was nothing there? Or maybe there was—you could feel it—but you couldn't see it. The results didn't quite pan out.

These are tough realities for the best of us, but for Ph.D. students betting their latent careers on a single project, they are terrifying. I have seen more than one Ph.D. project come crashing down because data carefully collected and analyzed revealed little of interest.

For a long time I thought this uncertainty was a normal part of the research process. I even tried to convince myself that there was something exciting about not knowing whether a study would bear fruit. But, in truth, there is nothing exciting about wasting years of work. It's frustrating in the extreme.

Then I stumbled upon meta-analysis and the all-important concept of effect size. That, in turn, led me to the analysis of statistical power.

It was like somebody had switched on all the lights.

I began to understand that much of the uncertainty I had lived with was nothing more than ignorance on my part. Like an investor buying shares in the Titanic, I was setting myself up to fail.

I was both thrilled to discover power analysis and saddened that I hadn't learned this stuff sooner. None of my methods teachers and none of the methods books on my shelf said anything about it. The few texts that did mention it struck me as unnecessarily dense and hard to read.

Rather than curse the darkness I decided to light a candle, so I wrote my own book; *The Essential Guide to Effect Sizes: Statistical Power, Meta-Analysis, and the Interpretation of Research Results*. It's a comprehensive yet jargon-free introduction to the largely ignored subject of effect sizes and their role in meta- and statistical power analysis.

When my book came out I set up a promotional website called www.effectsizefaq.com. The site has helpful tips and tricks along with links to useful resources such as online calculators. The site has proven quite popular attracting millions of page views.

By monitoring traffic on the site, I have discovered that researchers and students are looking for straight-forward answers to three important questions:

(1) What is an effect size?

(2) How do I calculate the statistical power of my study?

(3) How do I draw definitive conclusions from inconclusive studies?

The book you are reading answers the second question. Two other books in the MadMethods series, *Effect Size Matters* and *Meta-Analysis Made Easy*, answer the first and third questions respectively. (Value tip: You get three-books-in-one for a low price in the omnibus version.)

If you are unfamiliar with the concept of effect sizes, I recommend reading the first one before diving into this one. A good understanding of effect sizes and how to measure them is an essential precursor to power analysis. And if you wish to learn how to harvest effect sizes from past research, the third book provides a step-by-step guide.

Why did I write these books when I have already written a perfectly good text? Because students are poor and researchers are busy. You probably don't have six months to come to grips with these new subjects. You just want the short version.

Voila!

This book is designed to be a quick and easy introduction to the analysis of statistical power. By the time you're done, you should be able to run power analyses and design studies with sufficient power to detect the effects you are seeking. You will be attuned to the very real threat of Type II errors, and you will be equipped to deal with this risk.

Paul D. Ellis

What is statistical power? And how can I get some?

Let's begin with a plain-English definition:

> Statistical power describes the probability that a statistical test will correctly identify a genuine effect.

By genuine effect I mean an effect that is real as opposed to imaginary. For instance, if smoking has an effect on lung cancer, a properly empowered test should be able to detect this effect. If smoking has no effect lung cancer, then all the statistical power in the world won't help you prove that it does.

Statistical power will not help you see things that aren't there but it will help you see things that are. Like the magnification power in binoculars, the more statistical power you have, the easier it is to see things.

As long as the effect you are looking for is genuine — meaning, it exists in the real world — a study with sufficient statistical power will have a good chance of detecting it. Indeed, the probability of detection is directly proportional to statistical power. But what does it mean to detect effects? This leads to a question that should be asked in introductory stats course but often isn't...

How do we prove things with statistics?

It would be nice if someone invented a Geiger-counter-type box that you could point at your data and that clicked if there was something there. *Click, click, click—there's a bona fide result in there!*

Better still would be a Starfleet-issued tricorder that could detect evidence of real effects hidden in your database.

Imagine how interesting the Results sections of our papers would be!

Since there are no such effect-detection devices, we have to rely on ancient tools and practices devised by dead statisticians. The most famous of these is the p value which has its origins in work done by Sir Ronald Fisher in the 1920s.

Part A: The Analysis of Statistical Power

Sir Ronald understood that people are very good at looking at the evidence and jumping to the wrong conclusions.

- We pass a white cop who has stopped a black driver and, unaware that the driver has been speeding, we conclude the cop is engaging in racial profiling.
- We notice a colleague arriving late to the office and, unaware that they have just pulled an all-nighter, we assume they are slacking off.
- We ask an overweight friend, "When is the baby due?"

Humans are so good at seeing things that are not there, that we have a name for these sorts of mistakes. We call them Type I errors, a.k.a. false positives, a.k.a. crying wolf.

Sir Ronald wisely decided that researchers need insurance against drawing unsubstantiated conclusions, so he got a hammer and chisel and carved into the proverbial stone the number point-oh-five. If you have ever wondered where the critical p value of .05 comes from, you can thank Fisher (1925).

What does .05 represent? It is the benchmark level of probability we must exceed before we are permitted to draw conclusions from our data. Fisher argued that results which fall below this arbitrary threshold could be considered statistically significant while all others should be viewed with circumspection.

How do we prove things with statistics? You may recall from your Stats 101 course that for every hypothesized effect there is an opposing hypothesis called the null. The null hypothesis is always that the effect size equals zero:

- null hypothesis: there is no effect (the effect size = 0)
- alternative hypothesis: there is some effect (the effect size ≠ 0)

Now this is where it gets a little weird. While we may be interested in, say, the effect of smoking on lung cancer, what we actually test with our stats is something quite different: we test the null. In other words, we test the hypothesis that there is no effect, that smoking *doesn't* cause lung cancer.

Using probability theory, we run statistical tests to determine the likeliness of our result *assuming the null is true*. In other words, if there was no effect, how likely is the result we are seeing? The outcome of this test is the observed probability, the famous p value, which decides the fate of our test results (and indirectly, our careers!).

Fisher actually called for researchers to examine different types of evidence when testing hypotheses but history seems to have forgotten that. What we do instead, is bet the farm on the p.

For instance, if I find evidence of a link between smoking and lung cancer and the p value for my test result is < .05, I'll shout, "I found something! Fame and glory, here I come." But if my p value ≥ .05, I'll bang my head against the desk in despair. "There's nothing here! I've wasted the best years of my life on this dud project."

If you think there is something strange about my reaction to the p value, you'd be right.

One could argue that the evidence, namely, my esti-mate of the effect size, stands independently of the p value. By focusing on the results of my statistical significance tests, I am missing the really important thing, which is the evidence itself.[6]

Yet such is the state of research that many test results live and die on an arbitrary benchmark set by Fisher. If our test returns a $p < .05$, we stamp our results "statistically significant," pop champagne corks, and tell ourselves, "Congratulations. You found something."

---

[6] Effect sizes are the bread and butter of research. They constitute the evidence of our studies and are the reason why we do what we do. If you are not familiar with effect sizes and how they differ from test statistics like p and t, check out my MadMethods book, *Effect Size Matters*.

Why do Type I errors get all the attention?

You probably learned the difference between Type I and II errors in your first stats course. If you've forgotten, here's a reminder:

- Type I error — seeing things that aren't there
- Type II error — not seeing things that are there

Which error is more embarrassing? According to Sir Ron, Type I errors are the ones to avoid. Far better to skeptically dismiss things that are real than to foolishly accept things that are not.

Since the probability of making either error ranges from 0 (no chance) to 1 (dead certain), Sir Ron decided to set the tolerance level for Type I errors at .05, just a touch above 0. This begs the question, why not set the level of acceptable risk at zero? Why risk *any* Type I errors?

There is a good reason. If we set the cut-off at zero, then none of our results would ever achieve statistical significance and we wouldn't be able to use inferential stats to detect effects.

Setting the cut-off at $p = .00$ is like blinding yourself because you don't want to see cat videos. Now you might have good reasons for disliking cat videos, but I'm sure you would agree that nothing is worth blindness.

It's the same situation here.

If we never risked Type I errors we would make plenty of Type II errors because the two are related. Shut your eyes to avoid Type I errors and you'll invariably make a Type II error. You'll miss things that are worth seeing.

Scientists and researchers are paid to look for things. But if Sir Ron is to be believed, it is better to look with squinty-eyed skepticism than wide-eyed naiveté. "Look, but don't believe everything you see," he might've said. "Cultivate a near-zero tolerance for Type I errors."

Judging by the high esteem held for the mighty p, most scholars would agree.

What are four outcomes of any statistical test?

Since there are two types of error — seeing things that aren't there and not seeing things that are — there are four possible outcomes to any test of statistical significance. If there is no effect in the real world, we will either come to the correct conclusion or we will wrongly conclude there is an effect when there isn't (a Type I error). Conversely, if there is an effect, we will either come to the correction conclusion or we will wrongly conclude that there is no effect when there is (a Type II error).

These four outcomes are represented in Figure 1.

You may be wondering about the α and β symbols in the Figure. These Greek letters refer to alpha and beta respectively. Before we jump into power analysis, we need to learn a little bit about both.

I promise you, this will be the only time we do any Greek in this book.

Figure 1: Four test outcomes

What is true in the real world?

What conclusion is reached?	There is no effect (null = true)	There is an effect (null = false)
No effect	Correct conclusion ($p = 1 - \alpha$)	Type II error ($p = \beta$)
An effect	Type I error ($p = \alpha$)	Correct conclusion ($p = 1 - \beta$)

What are alpha and beta?

- alpha (α) = the probability of making a Type I error
- beta (β) = the probability of making a Type II error

There, that wasn't too hard was it?

There are two things to note about alpha and beta. First, they are mathematically related. As one goes down the other goes up. So when Sir Ronald says, "I can't bear the thought of making a Type I error," he is implicitly saying, "Type II errors I can live with." He's saying, "I strongly prefer beta to alpha."

The second thing to note about alpha and beta is they are both conditional probabilities; alpha is the conditional probability of making an error *when the null hypothesis is true*, while beta is the conditional probability of making an error *when the null hypothesis is false*.

Which means you are only ever in danger of making one error, not both.

This is one of those things that is so obviously true that many people don't see it. To repeat: the null cannot be true and false at the same time.

Either...

- the null is true (there is no effect) and you cannot make a Type II error, or
- the null is false (there is an effect) and you cannot make a Type I error

Consequently, in any given test only one type of error is possible. You are either risking a Type I error or a Type II error. The problem is we often don't know which error we are risking. When we don't know in advance whether the null is true or false, it is a good idea to insure against both types of error, with most of our insurance going towards errors of the first type.

But what happens when we have prior reasons for believing that an effect really does exist?

Let's say we have years of research testifying to the existence of an effect. In this case it seems pointless insuring against Type I errors since there is no chance—absolutely none at all—of making a Type I error.

The effect *is* real.

The null *is* false.

The only error we can make is a Type II error. The only way we can screw this up is by concluding there is no effect when, in fact, there is.

And how might we make this error? We draw a bad conclusion from a statistically nonsignificant result. This leads to our next question…

What is the wrong way to interpret a statistically nonsignificant result?

A researcher runs a test, gets a statistically nonsignificant result, and concludes, "There is no effect. There is no link, no relationship, no evidence that X affects Y." This is the wrong way to interpret a nonsignificant result. The absence of evidence is not evidence of absence.

A statistically nonsignificant result is an inconclusive result; it could mean there is no effect, or there is an effect but the test lacked the statistical power to detect it. We can't tell which it is by looking at the p value. If there is an effect and you conclude there isn't one, then you've made a Type II error. Publish your result and you'll misdirect future research. It would have been better for all concerned if you had not done the study at all.

As we will see, Type II errors of this type are the bane of the social sciences. They arise because researchers don't know how to distinguish effect sizes from p values and because they give no thought to the statistical power of their studies.

The tradeoff between alpha and beta is a big thorny debate that takes us places we don't need to go in this primer. What you do need to know is that while alpha has received all the attention for the past 90–odd years, there is a growing recognition of the need to sensibly manage beta.

This leads us to the next question...

How much power is enough?

Statistical power describes the probability that a test will correctly identify a real effect. (Here we are referring to the box in the lower right corner of Figure 1 above.) How much power should we aim for? If there is an effect to be found, what sort of chance do we want to give ourselves of finding it?

Obviously we would like to have a 100 percent chance of detecting an effect, but to achieve that might require considerable resources.

Imagine you are researching a cure for diabetes and you have developed a promising drug. You want to run a test to find out whether the drug is an effective treatment. One way to know with absolute certainty is to test every diabetes patient on the planet. Give half of them the drug and the rest a placebo in a double-blind trial and then watch what happens.

The beauty of this is approach is that you won't need inferential statistics. Since you are conducting a census instead of relying on a sample, you can simply count heads. If more people recover in the treatment group than the control group, the cure works.

The problem with this approach is it's prohibitively expensive. Close to 400 million people suffer from diabetes. Involving all of them in a trial would not only cost a fortune, it would divert resources away from other potential cures. We ought to be trialing multiple treatments and not betting all our money on just one horse.

So for lots of good reasons we rely on samples and live with a little uncertainty. But how much uncertainty is the right amount? Thanks to Fisher and a century of research practice, we have a rock-solid convention for managing alpha, but what about beta? Is there a conventional level of risk we should be prepared to accommodate when dealing with the threat of Type II errors? There is.

Jacob Cohen (1988) argued that studies should have no more than a 20 percent probability of making a Type II error. Why 20 percent? There's no special reason other than it seems to strike a nice balance between alpha and beta risk. Cohen reasoned that most researchers would view Type I errors as being four times more serious than Type II errors and therefore deserving of more stringent safeguards. Thus, if alpha significance levels are set at .05, then beta levels should be set at .20.

Since statistical power is the probability of detecting an effect when there is an effect to be detected, power can be quantified as the inverse of beta:

$$\text{Statistical power} = 1 - \beta$$

Shooting for a 20 percent risk of beta means designing studies such that they have an 80 percent probability of detecting real effects. Cohen provides the rationale:

> A materially smaller value than .80 would incur too great a risk of a Type II error. A materially larger value would result in a demand for N that is likely to exceed the investigator's resources. (Cohen 1992: 156)

Now that we have learned how statistical significance tests are used to make inferences about real world effects, we can finally turn to the analysis of statistical power.

What is power analysis for?

The analysis of statistical power is useful for answering questions like these:

1. How big a sample size do I need to test my hypotheses?
2. I only have access to 40 (or 100 or 15) cases—do I have enough power to test my hypotheses?
3. Assuming the phenomenon I'm searching for is real, what are my chances of finding it given my research design? And how I can increase my chances?

Sticking with our diabetes example, let's say you want to test your drug but you only have access to 40 patients. Is this sample going to be big enough to reveal the effects of your treatment? This is the sort of question that power analysis can answer.

Remember, there are two separate issues here: Either your drug has an effect or it doesn't and either you will conclude that it does or you won't. Each issue requires a different set of skills. The efficacy of your drug will depend on your skills as a drug-maker; the veracity of your conclusions will reflect your skills as a power-analyst.

See the difference?

Power analysis won't help you invent a cure for diabetes. Nor will it help you design an effective strategy, an intervention, a crisis response, an advertising campaign, or any sort of treatment.

But power analysis will help you design and interpret a test which reveals the effectiveness of whatever it is you're testing. It will alert you to the degree of threat posed by a Type II error. And since you have invested resources in what may be a cure for diabetes (or a brilliant strategy, ad-campaign, or whatever), a Type II error is something you definitely don't want to make.

What factors affect statistical power?

Studies vary in their levels of statistical power. Other things equal, a study with a large sample has more power than a study with a small sample. But sample size is just one of four parameters used in power analysis:

1. The **alpha significance criterion** (α) quantifies the risk of committing a Type I error and is conventionally set to a threshold level of .05.

2. The **sample size** or number of observations (N) determines the sampling error and affects the sensitivity of the test. The greater the N the greater the power.

3. The **effect size** (ES) describes the degree to which the phenomenon is present in the population. The larger the effect, the easier it is to detect and the greater the power of the test.

4. **Statistical power** quantifies the chosen Type II error rate (β) and is defined as $1 - \beta$. Ideally, the probability of avoiding Type II errors will be at least .80.

How to analyze statistical power and when

The four parameters of power analysis are mathematically related. This means the value of any parameter can be determined from the other three.

For instance, if the effect size is small, the sample size is small, and the critical level of alpha is low or stringent, then the resulting power will be low. Why? Because small effects are easy to miss, small samples are more likely to generate sampling errors, and stringent alphas make it harder for researchers to draw conclusions about the effects they may be seeing.

Conversely, if the effect size is big, the sample is large, and the alpha significance criterion is relaxed, statistical power will be high. Why? Because big effects in big samples are easier to see, especially when you're not too worried about the threat of Type I errors.

The relationship between the four parameters of power analysis can be expressed as follows:

$N \rightarrow \quad$ ES $\quad \leftarrow \alpha$ If you know the sample
$\qquad\qquad \uparrow$ size, the desired power
$\qquad$ Power   and alpha, you can
                                    calculate the minimum
                                    effect size detectable with
                                    your test.

ES $\rightarrow \quad$ N $\quad \leftarrow \alpha$ If you know the effect size,
$\qquad\qquad \uparrow$ the desired power, and the
$\qquad$ Power   alpha, you can calculate
                                    the required sample size.

ES $\rightarrow \quad$ Power $\quad \leftarrow \alpha$ If you know the effect size,
$\qquad\qquad \uparrow$ the sample size, and the
$\qquad\qquad N$ alpha, you can calculate
                                    the statistical power of
                                    your test and quantify the
                                    threat of Type II errors.

Why are these things good to know?

If you knew prior to conducting a study that you had, at best, only a 20 percent chance of getting a statistically significant result, would you proceed with the study? Or how would you like to know in advance the minimum sample size required to have a decent chance of detecting the effect you are studying? These are the sorts of questions that power analysis can answer.

Consider the following examples:

- If you have a sample of $N = 60$ and anticipate an effect size equivalent to $r = .25$, a quick power calculation would reveal that you have less than a 50 percent chance of obtaining a statistically significant result using a two-tailed test with alpha set at the conventional level of .05. *A 50:50 chance?! I don't like those odds. This project's a dead duck.*

- However, if you were able to double the size of your sample, the probability that your results will turn out to be statistically significant—assuming the effect you're searching for actually exists— rises to nearly 80 percent. *Oh, that's much better. I'm sure I can get the extra funding I need to keep this project alive.*

Now we begin to understand why Cohen said he felt like he had died and gone to heaven when he stumbled on to power analysis. It's like getting a crystal ball and determining whether your results are going to pan out *before you've begun the study!*

When is the best time to do a power analysis?

Ideally, a power analysis should be run before a study is conducted. Such an analysis is prospective in nature. Its purpose is to help us make informed judgments before we commit resources to a new project.

Prospective analyses of statistical power can be used to determine minimum detectable effect sizes, required sample sizes, and the likelihood of making Type II errors given other factors. Let's see how this works in practice with reference to our diabetes drug example...

How do I calculate the minimum detectable effect size?

We have 40 patients, we decide to follow convention and set alpha at .05, and we agree with Cohen that 0.80 is a desirable level of statistical power (meaning, we are prepared to tolerate, at worst, a 20 percent chance of making a Type II error). Given these three parameters, what is the smallest effect size we will be able to detect in our study?

Effects come in two families; the d-family and the r-family. Since in this study we are likely to be comparing a treatment group with a control group (with 20 in each group), we will measure effects using metrics from the d-family.

To calculate the minimum effect size, we might consult a table such as Table 1:

Table 1: Minimum detectable effect sizes

Sample size	d		r	
	One-tailed	Two-tailed	One-tailed	Two-tailed
10	1.72	2.02	.70	.76
20	1.16	1.32	.53	.58
30	.93	1.06	.44	.48
40	.80	.91	.38	.43
50	.71	.81	.34	.38
60	.65	.74	.31	.35
70	.60	.68	.29	.33
80	.56	.63	.27	.31
90	.53	.60	.26	.29
100	.50	.57	.25	.28

Source: Adapted from Ellis (2010b, Table 3.2).
Note: alpha = .05, power = .80

This table tells us that for a pooled sample size of 40 patients, the minimum detectable effect size in the d

metric when using two-tailed tests is .91. This is a huge effect size. To put it in context, the effect of the beta-blocker propranolol on survival rates for heart attacks is a much smaller $d = .08$ (Kolata 1981).

What does this mean? Our power analysis reveals that unless we have some fantastic wonder-drug on our hands, any results we get are unlikely to achieve statistical significance. Sadly, we doubt that our drug is a miracle cure. In fact, we have good reasons to suspect its effect might be rather small.

(Most effects are small. Small doesn't necessarily mean trivial since small effects may lead to note-worthy improvements in health or add up to large consequences.)

If we are dealing with a small effect, a sample size of 40 is not going to be much use. By that I mean, a small effect is unlikely to register as statistically significant because our study lacks power. Okay. So assuming the effect *is* small, how big a sample would we need? This leads us to our next question...

How do I calculate the required sample size?

Based on the evidence of past research we have good reasons to anticipate an effect size of $d = .20$. To calculate the minimum sample size needed to detect such an effect given conventional levels of alpha and power, we might consult a table such as Table 2. The left-hand columns of the table show us the minimum sample sizes required for a range of effect sizes in the d metric; the right-hand columns provide sample sizes for a range of effect sizes in the r metric.

Table 2: Minimum sample sizes

ES = d	N	ES = r	N
.10	3,142	.05	3,137
.20	<u>787</u>	.10	782
.30	351	.15	346
.40	199	.20	193
.50	128	.25	123
.60	90	.30	84
.70	67	.35	61
.80	52	.40	46
.90	41	.45	36
1.00	34	.50	29

Source: Adapted from Ellis (2010b, Table 3.1).
Notes: The sample sizes reported for d are pooled (i.e., $n_1 + n_2$), $\alpha_2 = .05$, power $= .80$

Table 2 tells is that for an effect size equivalent to $d = 0.2$, we will need a sample size of at least $N = 787$ to have an 80 percent chance of detection (or a 20 percent chance of avoiding a Type II error).

In other words, to detect a small effect you need a big sample.[7]

And if you plan on doing subgroup or multivariate analyses, you'll need a bigger sample still.

Minimum sample sizes should be based on the size of the smallest group to be tested or on the number of predictors in your model.[8]

_____

[7] If you decide to verify these numbers with a computer program such as G*Power 3, you will get a minimum sample size of 788, not 787. Which is correct? They both are. The sample sizes in Table 2 are pooled, meaning, you have to cut them in half to figure out how many in each of your comparison groups. Half of 787 is 393.5. Since you can't put 393.5 people into a group, the safe bet is to round up and have 394. If you have two groups of 394, your combined sample size is 788, which is the number that G*Power 3 gives you.
[8] Since it is beyond the scope of this short guide to delve into these issues, the interested reader is directed to Green (1991) and Kelley and Maxwell (2008).

How do I calculate the statistical power of my study?

Clearly, 40 patients isn't going to cut it. If we proceed with such a small sample the probability of making a Type II error runs as high as 91 percent. Continue with the study as is, and we are setting ourselves up for almost certain failure (if by "fail" we mean fail to reach a conclusive result).

Wait, slow down.

How did I arrive at this figure of 91 percent?

On this occasion, I didn't consult a table but I used a program called G*Power 3. Figure 2 provides a screenshot.

This program is a powerful tool suited to running a variety of power analyses. You can download it for free from a site maintained by the University of Dusseldorf (see Faul *et al.*, 2007, 2009).

Figure 2: Calculating power with G*Power 3

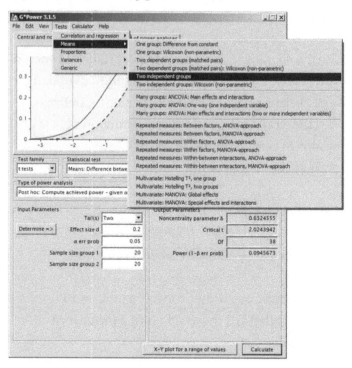

To learn how G*Power 3 works, download the free user-guide when you install the program, but here are the steps I followed to determine the likelihood of a Type II error in our diabetes example:

1. From the menu bar at the top of the app I selected Tests>Means>Two independent groups

2. Under "Type of Power Analysis," I selected "Post hoc"

3. I inputted the following parameters:
    o   for "Tail(s)" I entered two (indicating a two-tailed test)
    o   for "Effect size d" I entered 0.2
    o   I left the "α err prob" unchanged at 0.05
    o   for "Sample size group 1" I entered 20 and I did the same for "Sample size group 2"

4. I then pressed "Calculate" and got the numbers you see in the screenshot

The number of interest is found in the box on the lower right-hand corner:

$$\text{Power } (1-\beta \text{ err prob}) = 0.0945673$$

This is the power of our study. Since power equals 1 - β, then beta (the probability of making a Type II error) equals 1 - 0.0945673 or 0.91.

So far all our examples have been in the d metric, but what if we wanted to run power analyses for effects measured in the correlational or r metric? It's the same basic process. The tables above along with those you'll find in power texts generally provide two sets of figures, one for each metric. As long as you can tell d from r you won't have any problems. Similarly, G*Power 3 provides the full gamut of tests for the r metric. Here's a worked example…

How do I calculate sample size using G*Power 3?

Say you want to do a study assessing the link between exposure to tobacco smoke and the risk of lung cancer. You have reason to believe that the correlation between these two variables is equivalent to $r = .30$. (How do you know this? You did a meta-analysis or ran a pre-test.) How big a sample would you need to test for an effect of this size?

1. From the menu bar at the top of G*Power 3 select Tests>Correlation and regression>Correlation: bivariate normal model

2. Under "Type of Power Analysis" select "A priori: Compute required sample size"

3. Input the following parameters:
     o for "Tail(s)" enter two (indicating a two-tailed test)
     o for "Correlation ϱ H1" enter 0.3

- o leave "α err prob" unchanged at 0.05
- o for Power (1 − β err prob) enter 0.8
- o leave "Correlation ϱ H0" unchanged at 0
  (this is the null hypothesis)

4. Press "Calculate" and you should end up with the numbers you see in the screenshot shown in Figure 3.

The output of interest is in the cell marked "Total sample size." The result tells us that we need a minimum sample size of $N = 84$ if we are to have an 80 percent probability of detecting an effect size equivalent to $r = 0.3$.

(Just for fun, you can cross-check these numbers with Table 2 above.)

But what if we decided to run a directional or one-tailed test instead? After all, there is considerable evidence to show that exposure to tobacco smoke has an adverse effect on lung health. There is not a lot of debate over the direction of the effect. Smoking doesn't make you healthy.

Figure 3: Calculating sample size with G*Power 3

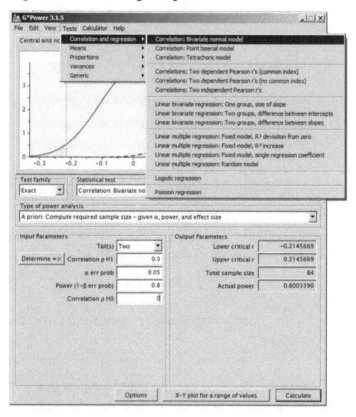

In this case we could rerun the analysis after selecting "One" in the box next to "Tails." Switching from a two-tailed to a one-tailed test boosts statistical power as evidenced by a corresponding drop in the required sample size. This time we only need $N = 67$ to achieve the same level of power as before.

Clear as mud?

If you would like a little more practice analyzing statistical power or calculating sample sizes, check out the bonus exercises in Appendix 1.

Why are most effects small?

In the examples we've just done, we have had a prior expectation about the size of the effect, but in practice, we often have no idea. We're in the dark. If you don't know the size of the effect you are looking for, set your expectations low. Chances are, it's small. Really small.

Why do I say this?

Results are like gold nuggets—the big ones get picked up first. The pioneers in any new field of inquiry get to pluck the low-hanging fruit. What remains for those who follow are the crumbs. (I hope you like mixed metaphors!)

For a long time I had a nagging suspicion that the majority of effects in the social sciences are small. However, when I looked at the evidence in my own field, I was amazed to find that the majority of effects are actually smaller than small—they're tiny.

Here's how I came to that conclusion.

Wanting to identify some typical effect sizes in the field of international business, I scanned 32 journals to identify every meta-analysis published in a 15–year period.[9] My search led to the identification of 23 meta-analyses that collectively accounted for a combined sample of $N = 223,800$ (see Ellis 2010a).

Here is what I found: Of the 23 mean effect sizes reported in the meta-analyses,

- five would be regarded as small in terms of Cohen's (1992) effect size conventions (i.e., $.10 \leq r < .30$)
- eighteen would be regarded as smaller than small (i.e., $r < .10$)

Figure 4 portrays the 23 mean effect sizes graphically. It should be obvious from this figure that typical effect sizes in international business are not very big.

---

[9] What is a meta-analysis? A meta-analysis is where you pool the results of available research to calculate a weighted, mean estimate of effect size. A meta-analysis can help you identify the effect size you need to run a power analysis. Conducting a meta-analysis is not hard. As I explain in my MadMethods book, *Meta-Analysis Made Easy*, you can learn the basics in less than an hour.

In fact, the weighted mean of the 23 weighted mean effect sizes was just $r = .06$. That is tiny, some might say, even trivial in size.

In percentage of variance terms it means that the average effect size is equivalent to less than half of one percent.

International business researchers have it tough!

These results are not unusual. Meta-analyses done in other social science disciplines routinely report effect sizes that are small in size (e.g., Mazen *et al.*, 1987).

We all have it tough!

What do we do with this information?

The best response is make sure our studies are sufficiently empowered to detect small effects.

Figure 4: Mean effect sizes in international business research

Notes: Effect sizes are expressed in absolute values. AM = Abumustafa and Mohamed (2009), BK = Bausch and Krist (2007), Bor = Borkowski (1996), Mag = Magnusson, *et al.*, (2008), RR = Reus and Rottig (2009), Sho = Shoham (2003), TGR = Tihanyi, Griffith and Russell (2005), ZLS = Zhao, Luo and Suh (2004)

Part A: The Analysis of Statistical Power

Say the effect you are searching for is equivalent to r = .06. Under conventional levels of alpha and power, you will need a sample size of at least 2,177 to detect such a small effect. If you decide to relax your statistical significance standards by opting for one-tailed rather than two-tailed tests, you will still need an N of at least 1,716 to give yourself an 80 percent chance of getting a statistically significant result.

These are big sample sizes, bigger, I suspect, than the majority of those found in the social sciences. This leads to our next question...

The dangers of an under-powered study

Hopefully by now the answer to this question is obvious. The lower the power, the greater the probability you won't find anything. Or rather, the greater the likelihood you'll get an inconclusive result.

There is a two-fold risk here. First, in any low-powered study, the estimate of the effect size is likely to be tainted by sampling error. How can you be sure that your small sample is not quirky in some unpredictable way? There is a reason pollsters survey thousands rather than dozens of people, and that is to reduce the margin of error in their results.

Second, if your study lacks statistical power, there is a greater chance of making a Type II error. This happens because the smaller your sample, the greater the likelihood that your results will turn out to be statistically nonsignificant. A nonsignificant result is *not* a Type II error but it can lead to one.

How does low statistical power lead to Type II errors?

This point is worth repeating: Low power leads to statistically nonsignificant results and a nonsignificant result is an *inconclusive* result. It might mean there is no effect, or there is an effect but the test lacked the statistical power to detect it.

If you interpret a statistically nonsignificant result as evidence of no effect, and there really is an effect, then you will have made a Type II error.

My study is under-powered, how can I increase statistical power?

As we will see in Part B, most studies done are woefully under-powered. They lack the power to detect sought-after effects and so run a high risk of generating Type II errors. In many cases there is a clear need for more power. How can we get it? Here are five ways:

1. Increase the sample size

The size of your sample will likely have the biggest effect on the statistical power of your study. So to increase power, increase N. In some cases doubling the N will lead to a greater than doubling of statistical power, but not always. In a few situations increasing the N will have only a marginal effect on statistical power. The point is not to throw money at the problem but to determine your ideal sample size by analyzing the trade-off between sampling costs, which are additive, and the corresponding gains in power, which may be incremental and diminishing.

2. Search for bigger effects

Tighter relationships are easier to spot than mediated or moderated relationships, so one way to increase power is to look for outcomes that are closely related to treatments (or dependent variables that are closely related to predictors).

3. Reduce measurement error

Unreliable measures are like dirty lenses on telescopes—they make it harder to see what you're looking for.

It is beyond the scope of this short book to examine the relationship between measurement error and statistical power but it's not a happy one.

Measurement error is like a leech sucking the power out of your study.[10]

4. Choose appropriate statistical tests for the data

Parametric tests are more powerful than non-parametric tests; directional (one-tailed) tests are more powerful than non-directional (two-tailed) tests; and tests involving metric data are more powerful than tests involving nominal or ordinal data.

5. Relax the alpha significance criterion (α)

Take a hammer and smash those stone tablets of Fisher's. Yes, you will run into institutional opposition—the .05 is held sacred by many. But a thoughtful researcher should be able to make a good argument for relaxing alpha in settings where the risk of a Type II error is greater than the risk of a Type I error. It won't be easy to convince reviewers, but you could try.

---

[10] To learn more about the leech and how to kill it, see Ellis 2010b, chapter 3.

The dangers of an over-powered study

Hopefully it is clear by now that under-powered studies are generally not worth doing. If there isn't a good chance of finding what you're looking for, why waste resources looking for it? The temptation then might be to pursue as much power as possible. But over-powered studies are not without dangers of their own.

Consider a study with a sample size of 5,000. Without running a power analysis we can safely conclude that such a study has tons of power and it does. In fact, it will be powerful enough to detect effects as small as r = .04. The question is, are such effects worth detecting? In some settings they might be, but most of the time effects of this size are rightly dismissed as trivial, barely real, and possibly reflecting nothing more than background noise in the database.

I recently came across a study in a top tier journal that was based on a panel dataset of 117,000 observations. The results table looked like a conference for asterisks. Or a map of the night sky. Not only was everything statistically significant, but most results were significant at the $p < .01$ level. It was quite a sight.

Now there is nothing wrong with having lots of statistically significant results. The problem was the authors interpreted all of their results as though they were *practically* significant. In other words, they confused statistical with substantive significance. Such is the mindless adherence to the sacred .05 that none of the reviewers picked this up.

If these authors had examined their effect sizes directly, they would have dismissed a lot of their statistically significant results as trivial. For instance, one of their results was so small that it in proportion of variance terms the predictor accounted for 1/25th of one percent of the variance in the outcome variable. That's what you call a nothing effect. It's the weight of your shadow. It's the sound of an eyelid closing. However, distracted by their rash of asterisks (indicating low p values), the authors missed the utter trivialness of this effect and interpreted the test result as evidence in support of their hypothesis. It wasn't.

To clarify, the problem is not one of having too much data—the more the better!—but in the possibly prodigal expenditure of resources. A study is wasteful to the degree to which the costs of collecting the data needed to estimate effects exceed the benefits of doing so.[11]

Why can't I draw substantive conclusions from p values?

It is not uncommon for researchers to draw conclusions about observed effects by examining p values generated by tests of significance. If a result is statistically significant, unwise authors will conclude conclude that the effect is real, big, and interesting.

---

[11] The use of secondary or published data can lead to samples that are phenomenally huge, such as Singh's (2007) analysis of 6.9m patent dyads. Another interesting trend is the growing number of studies done in China where large numbers seem to be the name of the game. The largest study based on primary data that I have come across is Hung *et al.*,'s (2007) analysis of market segments and consumer behavior in China. Their second sample ($N = 32,670$) drew on data obtained from a mix of interviews and self-administered surveys. Coincidentally, their study was published in the same issue as Singh's (2007) large N study making volume 38, issue 5 of the *Journal of International Business Studies* arguably the most statistically powerful journal issue of all time.

However, none of these conclusions is supported by the p value.

The p value is a confounded index. It changes in relation to the effect size *and* the sample size. If either one goes up p goes down. In many studies the biggest determinant of statistical power is sample size. Consequently, a p value usually says less about the size of the effect than the size of the sample from which it came.

Draw your conclusions from p values and you'll either risk missing small effects obtained in low-power settings (leading to a Type II error) or you'll make too much of trivial effects observed in high-power settings (leading to a Type I error). The best way to avoid either outcome is to interpret effect sizes independently of statistical significance tests.

My study is highly-powered, how can I avoid the dangers of misinterpretation?

Simple—don't draw substantive conclusions from p values. Instead, look at your estimate of the effect size and answer two questions: How big is it? And what does it mean?

Part A: The Analysis of Statistical Power

Interpreting statistical significance is easy; interpreting substantive significance is a different game entirely and one that requires you to think, to compare your estimates with those obtained from other studies, and to contextualize your results against a meaningful frame of reference.[12]

What is the tricky part of doing a power analysis?

If you are running a prospective power analysis, you're probably doing it because you want to know the required sample size. What's the catch? To calculate the sample size you need to know the effect size and that's probably the one thing you *don't* know (else why are you doing the study?).

It's a catch-22 situation: You can't design a good study without knowing the likely effect size and you can't know the effect size until you've done a good study!

Nor is this something you can afford to get wrong. Under-estimate the likely effect size and you will

---

[12] I provide tips and tricks on how to deal with the interpretation challenge in my MadMethods book *Effect Size Matters*.

over-state the required sample size, possibly to the point of killing the project. *We need how big a sample?! We can't afford that.* But over-estimate the effect size and the study may be under-powered and doomed to fail.

For these reasons it is essential that you have a fair idea of the expected effect size *before* you commit to a study. If you don't know how big the thing is that you're looking for, you won't know how much power you need to find it.

So where can you get good information on the likely effect size? You have three options:

1. refer to evidence of effect sizes reported in past research
2. make an estimate of the effect size based on theory
3. conduct a pre-test

A pre-test is always good idea, particularly if you plan on applying for a big research grant further down the track.

In our diabetes example we already have a sample of 40 patients ready to go. As we have seen, this sample size is not big enough to give us the definitive answers we are looking for. But if we use this group for a pre-test, we could learn plenty that will help us later on.

Here's how that could work.

We split the sample into two groups—a treatment group and a control group—and test our new drug. We measure the health of each group before and after the treatment and discover an improvement in the treatment group equivalent to $d = 0.55$. Unsurprisingly, a t-test reveals this result to be statistically nonsignificant.

Here's the wrong way to interpret that information:

Since our t-test revealed that the treatment had a statistically nonsignificant effect, we conclude the treatment doesn't work.

Why is that the wrong way? Because we don't know that the treatment doesn't work. All we know for sure is that with only 40 patients our study was never going to be capable of detecting anything less than whopper-sized effects. If our study has given us an accurate estimate of the effect size, we've just made a

Type II error and the one thing we should have known in advance was that the chances of that happening were high (60 percent, to be precise).

So what is the right way to interpret this result?

Our pretest revealed an improvement in the treatment group equivalent to $d = 0.55$ which we interpret as promising and worthy of further investigation. Based on estimates reporting in previous research, we anticipate the likely effect size to be in the $0.45 - 0.65$ range. Thus, we intend to seek funding for a larger study (N at least 158) to further test this treatment.

Same data, different conclusions. Go with the first conclusion and you'll kill a promising new drug. Go with the second conclusion and you may end up helping 400 million diabetes patients. You could win a Nobel Prize!

Is it too much of an exaggeration to say that the course and success of your career hinges on your ability to analyze statistical power?

What's wrong with retrospective power analyses?

So far we have looked at the situation where a power analysis is used to inform the design of future studies. But what about doing a power analysis after the fact? Say you do a study ad get a bunch of statistically nonsignificant results. You wonder, "What went wrong? Perhaps my study lacked power. Let's crunch the numbers to find out."

Beware! You are on the top of a slippery slope.

What is wrong with calculating power retrospectively? After all, isn't it reasonable to ask questions like:

- "My sample was too small; how big should it have been?"
- "Was insufficient power responsible for my nonsignificant result?"
- "What was the probability of making a Type II error in this study?"

These are fair questions and sometimes you will encounter journal editors who ask them. But calculating the power of a study based on the parameters of that study is fraught with danger.

The problem is this: observed effect sizes drawn from individual samples (especially small samples characterized by sampling error) are likely to be poor estimates of actual effect sizes. If you were to take the effect size estimate from your study and plug it into a retrospective power analysis, it would tell you nothing you didn't know and it would likely mislead you.

"But I got a statistically nonsignificant result," you might say. "I can't tell whether that means there is no effect or there is but my study lacked the power to detect it."

Again, this is a valid concern but a retrospective power analysis cannot help you resolve it. Take another look at Figure 1 above. Statistical power is only relevant in the right side of the table. It is only applies when the null is false. To calculate power after the fact is to make an assumption—the null is false—that is unsupported by the data. It's like trying to calculate an equation with two unknowns (Zumbo and Hubley 1998).

But what if we qualified our thoughts like this:

> I am going to assume the effect is real (or the null is false) because other research says so. I am further going to assume the effect size is the same as what I observed in my study. Under these circumstances, how big should my sample size have been given conventional levels of alpha and power?

There is nothing wrong with this question because it is prospective in nature. It is exactly the sort of question we might ask after a pre-test. Whether a power analysis based on these assumptions will generate good results or not hinges on how closely the effect size observed in the study reflects the true population effect size.

Intermission

In Part A we concerned ourselves with the basics of power analysis—why, how, and when to do it. Designing studies with statistical power in mind is one of the best ways to ensure research success.

So far we have limited our focus to the design of single studies. But researchers sometimes assess the statistical power of entire fields of study. They do this to gauge the prevalence of Type II errors and otherwise assess the statistical health of specific fields.

In Part B we will see that the results of these power surveys routinely reveal fatal flaws in published research.

The really bad news of power research

In the 1960s, Jacob Cohen had a brilliant idea: Why not calculate the average statistical power of all the studies published in the 1960 volume of *The Journal of Abnormal and Social Psychology*?

I know, it's a zinger of an idea. You're probably wondering, "Why didn't I think of that?"

Seriously, Cohen's idea was profoundly clever for it meant he could quantify, in cold, hard numbers, the prevalence of Type II errors in his field.

How did he do it?

Cohen recorded the sample sizes and test types for all 70 studies published in the 1960 volume and calculated average power for three hypothetical effect sizes. He found that the average power for detecting small, medium, and large effects was 0.18, 0.48, and 0.83 respectively.

These numbers are startling.

They tell us that unless the effects researchers were looking for were large, they had a greater chance of making a Type II error than getting a statistically significant result.

In other words, the majority of studies published in the 1960 volume of *The Journal of Abnormal and Social Psychology* were designed to be inconclusive.

Cohen's (1962) study was brilliant in its simplicity and stunning in its conclusions.

Almost immediately others started using his methods to calculate average power levels in fields such as education (Brewer 1972), communication (Kroll and Chase 1975), social work (Orme and Combs-Orme 1986), marketing research (Sawyer and Ball 1981), management (Mazen *et al.*, 1987), counseling research (Kosciulek and Szymanski 1993), and behavioral accounting (Borkowski *et al.*, 2001).

Following Cohen's lead, many of these surveys were limited to specific journals.

Which journals have had their statistical power assessed?

Part B: The Stunning Results of Power Research

Power analysts have attempted to gauge the average power of research published in the following 25 journals;

- Academy of Management Journal (Brock 2003; Cashen and Geiger 2004; Mazen *et al.*, 1987)
- Accounting Review (Lindsay 1993)
- Administrative Science Quarterly (Cashen and Geiger 2004; Mone *et al.*, 1996)
- American Educational Research Journal (Brewer 1972)
- Behavioral Research in Accounting (Borkowski *et al.*, 2001)
- British Journal of Psychology (Clark-Carter 1997)
- Decision Sciences (Baroudi and Orlikowski 1989)
- Journal of Abnormal Psychology (Rossi 1990)
- Journal of Abnormal and Social Psychology (Cohen 1962; Sedlmeier and Gigerenzer 1989)
- Journal of Accounting Research (Lindsay 1993)
- Journal of Applied Psychology (Chase and Chase 1976; Mone *et al.*, 1996)
- Journal of Clinical and Experimental Neuropsychology (Bezeau and Graves 2001)
- Journal of Consulting and Clinical Psychology (Rossi 1990)
- Journal of Information Systems (McSwain 2004)

- Journal of International Business Studies (Brock 2003; Ellis 2010a)
- Journal of Management (Cashen and Geiger 2004; Mazen *et al.*, 1987; Mone *et al.*, 1996)
- Journal of Management Accounting (Borkowski *et al.*, 2001)
- Journal of Management Information Systems (McSwain 2004)
- Journal of Management Studies (Cashen and Geiger 2004)
- Journal of Marketing Research (Sawyer and Ball 1981)
- Journal of Personality and Social Psychology (Rossi 1990)
- Management Sciences (Baroudi and Orlikowski 1989)
- MIS Quarterly (Baroudi and Orlikowski 1989)
- Neuropsychology (Bezeau and Graves 2001)
- Strategic Management Journal (Brock 2003; Cashen and Geiger 2004; Mone *et al.*, 1996)

The unanimous and overwhelming conclusion of these power surveys is that research across all social science disciplines is woefully underpowered. The typical study published in these journals lacked the power to detect anything except the largest of effect sizes (Ellis 2010b, Table 4.1). Since large effects are as rare as hen's teeth, the implications of this are sobering.

First, low power translates into an increased prevalence of Type II errors. Many studies are likely to be missing real effects simply because they lack the power to detect them.

Second, and somewhat surprisingly, low power across disciplines also translates into an increased prevalence of Type I errors. Not only are researchers missing things, they are seeing things that are not there. Consider these two contrasting facts:

-    with low average statistical power, the typical study in the social sciences has a small chance of finding anything
-    yet most published studies have found something, otherwise they would not have been published

How is this possible?

How is it that so many published studies have found something given that the odds of doing so were stacked against them?

There are two possible explanations. Either published studies routinely detect large effects (they don't) or authors of published studies are mistaking random variation in their samples for genuine effects (gulp!).

How does low statistical power lead to Type I errors?

In Part A we saw how low statistical power can lead to Type II errors. With insufficient power, you miss things. That much is obvious. But when low power is combined with publication policies favoring studies that find things over studies that don't, the paradoxical result is an increase in Type I errors.

How does this happen?

Recall that studies are purposely designed to balance the competing risks of Type I and Type II errors. Under normal circumstances this means that a small percentage of false positives is inevitable. In fact, for any set of studies about one in sixteen will be affected by Type I errors. That is, they will find things that don't exist.[13]

---

[13] These numbers are explained in Ellis 2010b, chapter 4.

Part B: The Stunning Results of Power Research

However, as average power levels fall, the proportion of false positives reported and published inevitably rises.

This happens because researchers sometimes fish in the data and engage in the sin of HARKing, or Hypothesizing After the Results are Known (Kerr 1998).

What is HARKing? And is it contagious?

HARKing is what you do when you stumble upon an unexpected result and then write the paper as if that result was your study's original object.

What's wrong with HARKing or fishing in the data?

The problem is your result is probably not real; it's a statistical fluke, an aberration in your sample. Run a large enough number of tests and the odds are good that something will turn out to be statistically significant, even if there's nothing there.

Imagine you've spent three long years on a study, crunched your numbers, and found... nothing. It's depressing. The temptation to play with the data is almost overwhelming. *There must be something here. I must find something to show for my labors.*

Well, run enough tests and you will find something. The probabilistic nature of null hypothesis significance testing guarantees that *something* will eventually turn out to be statistically significant even if there is *nothing* there.

So you play with the data, find a statistically significant result, and write a paper about it. "It must be real right? The p value says so." Wrong! What you have found is probably little more than a sampling quirk. You have a bona fide false positive. If you tried to replicate the result in a follow-up study, you would probably find that it did not exist.

But there's no time for that. It's publish or perish, up or out. So you write a compelling paper, fool a reviewer or two, and get a hit. Congratulations, you've just done bad science. You've reported something that's not real and misdirected future research on the topic.

For these reasons some scholars suspect that published results are more often wrong than right (e.g., Ioannidis 2005).

How can I avoid the temptation to HARK?

Rewriting papers to suit unexpected findings is a temptation some are unable to resist. How can we protect ourselves from the temptation to engage in a little bit of HARKing? What steps can we take to ensure we don't engage in this sort of bad science? There are at four things you can do:

Part B: The Stunning Results of Power Research

1. Design studies with adequate levels of power—not too little (or you won't see anything) or too much (or you will see everything; effects, quirks, sampling errors, random noise).

2. Don't fish in the dataset. Just don't. Let theory be your guide.

3. If you do stumble upon an unexpected result, label it as such—don't try and tell yourself that this is what you were looking for all along. Let others know that the result is unexpected and possibly dubious.

4. Validate your results through replication.

The main takeaway from this book

In this book we have learned that the majority of studies in the social sciences are fatally flawed by design, meaning, they are under-powered and unlikely to detect effects of interest. We have looked at five ways for increasing statistical power and we have discussed simple methods for computing minimum sample sizes and detectable effects. We have also learned why you cannot draw substantive conclusions from p values and why fishing in your dataset is a bad idea.

If I was to distill the single most important lesson of this book, it would be this: Consider statistical power when designing studies and running tests.

Studies which have too much or too little statistical power are inherently wasteful and potentially misleading. Even if researchers are careful to avoid making Type II errors, any underpowered study will lead to an inconclusive and therefore unsatisfactory result. For this reason the *Publication Manual* of the American Psychological Association makes the following recommendation:

When applying inferential statistics, take seriously the statistical power considerations associated with tests of the hypotheses. Such considerations relate to the likelihood of correctly rejecting the tested hypotheses, given a particular alpha level, effect size, and sample size. In that regard, routinely provide evidence that the study has sufficient power to detect effects of substantive interest. (APA 2010: 30)

"Provide evidence of sufficient power." Evidence in this context would be a prospective analysis of statistical power based on the anticipated effect size.

Prior expectations regarding the effect size should be informed either by theory or past research (including pre-tests) rather than effect sizes observed in the study itself. When researchers have little choice but to rely on small samples, statistical power considerations should motivate them to seek out large effects.

As we have seen, analyzing statistical power is not difficult. Anyone who can run a statistical test should be able to do a power analysis. Neither is power analysis time-consuming. Usually no more than an hour is needed. Given the potential benefits of analyzing power prior to starting projects that may run for years, it is an hour well spent.

Author's note

If you enjoyed *Statistical Power Trip*, would you mind posting a short customer review on Amazon? Doing so will help others find this book.

Thank you!

Appendix I: Bonus power exercises

Use either G*Power 3 or Tables 1 and 2 in this book to…

(a) calculate the required sample sizes for the following test conditions:

	ES metric	Effect size	Sample size
1.	d	0.60	
2.	d	0.10	
3.	d	0.70	
4.	d	0.40	
5.	d	0.30	
6.	r	0.45	
7.	r	0.05	
8.	r	0.20	
9.	r	0.25	
10.	r	0.10	

Note: alpha = .05, power = .80, all tests are two-tailed

(b) calculate the minimum detectable effect size for the following test conditions:

	Sample size	Test type	ES metric	Minimum detectable effect size
1.	80	1–tailed	d	
2.	20	1–tailed	d	
3.	50	2–tailed	r	
4.	100	1–tailed	r	
5.	40	2–tailed	d	
6.	90	2–tailed	r	
7.	60	1–tailed	d	
8.	10	2–tailed	r	
9.	30	2–tailed	r	
10.	70	2–tailed	d	

Note: alpha = .05, power = .80

Answers are on the following page.

Answers to exercises on the preceding page:

Exercise (a): (1) 90, (2) 3,142, (3) 67, (4) 199, (5) 351, (6) 36, (7) 3,137, (8) 193, (9) 123, (10) 782.
Exercise (b): (1) .56, (2) 1.16, (3) .38, (4) .25, (5) .91, (6) .29, (7) .65, (8) .76, (9) .48, (10) .68.

Note: Sample sizes for d are pooled (i.e., $n_1 + n_2$). When implementing the results of exercise (a) in the context of group comparisons, sample sizes with odd numbers should be rounded up to the nearest even number to permit equal numbers within each group.

Appendix 2: Ten great but slightly misquoted quotes about statistical power

"The measure of a man is what he does with *statistical* power."
> — Plato (424BC–348BC), Greek number cruncher

"An honest man can feel no pleasure in the exercise of *statistical* power over his fellow citizens."
> — Thomas Jefferson (1743–1826), third US President

"Only a man who knows what it is like to be defeated can reach down to the bottom of his soul and come up with the extra ounce of *statistical* power it takes to win when the match is even."
> — Muhammad Ali (1942–2016), professional boxer and *Sports Illustrated*'s Sportsman of the Century

"All things are subject to interpretation; whichever interpretation prevails at a given time is a function of *statistical* power and not truth."
> — Friedrich Nietzsche (1844–1900), German philosopher

"The day the power of love overrules the love of *statistical* power, the world will know peace."

> — Mahatma Gandhi (1869–1948),
> leader of Indian independence movement

"Being *statistically* powerful is like being a lady. If you have to tell people you are, you aren't."

> — Margaret Thatcher (1925–2013),
> Britain's first female prime minister

"Nearly all men can stand adversity, but if you want to test a man's character, give him *statistical* power."

> — Abraham Lincoln (1809–1865),
> sixteenth US President

"*Statistical* power is the ultimate aphrodisiac."

> — Henry Kissinger (1923–),
> former US Secretary of State

"*Statistical* power is my mistress. I have worked too hard at her conquest to allow anyone to take her away from me."

> — Napoleon Bonaparte (1769–1821), French Emperor

"With great *statistical* power, comes great responsibility."

> — Ben Parker, Spiderman's uncle

References

Abumustafa, N.I., and M.M. Mohamed (2009), "Do domestic firms benefit from multinational enterprises? A meta-analysis of the empirical research," *Journal of Transnational Management*, 14(1): 3–15.

APA (2010), Publication Manual of the American Psychological Association, 6th Edition. Washington DC: American Psychological Association.

Baroudi, J.J. and W.J. Orlikowski (1989), "The problem of statistical power in MIS research," *MIS Quarterly*, 13(1): 87–106.

Bausch, A., and M. Krist (2007), "The effect of context-related moderators on the internationalization-performance relationship: Evidence from meta-analysis," *Management International Review*, 47(3): 319–347.

Bezeau, S. and R. Graves (2001), "Statistical power and effect sizes of clinical neuropsychology research," *Journal of Clinical and Experimental Neuropsychology*, 23(3): 399–406.

Borkowski, S.C. (1996), "An analysis (meta- and otherwise) of multinational transfer pricing research," *International Journal of Accounting*, 31(1): 39–53.

Borkowski, S.C., M.J. Welsh, and Q. Zhang (2001), "An analysis of statistical power in behavioral accounting research," *Behavioral Research in Accounting*, 13: 63–84.

Brewer, J.K. (1972), "On the power of statistical tests in the American Educational Research Journal," *American Educational Research Journal*, 9(3): 391–401.

Brock, J. (2003), "The 'power' of international business research," *Journal of International Business Studies*, 34(1): 90–99.

Cashen, L.H. and S.W. Geiger (2004), "Statistical power and the testing of null hypotheses: A review of contemporary management research and recommendations for future studies," *Organizational Research Methods*, 7(2): 151–167.

Chase, L.J. and R.B. Chase (1976), "A statistical power analysis of applied psychological research," *Journal of Applied Psychology*, 61(2): 234–237.

Clark-Carter, D. (1997), "The account taken of statistical power in research published in the British Journal of Psychology," *British Journal of Psychology*, 88(1): 71–83.

Cohen, J. (1962), "The statistical power of abnormal-social psychological research: A review," *Journal of Abnormal and Social Psychology*, 65(3): 145–153.

Cohen, J. (1988), Statistical Power for the Behavioral Analysis, 2nd Edition. Hillsdale: Lawrence Erlbaum.

Cohen, J. (1990), "Things I have learned (so far)," *American Psychologist*, 45(12): 1304–1312.

Cohen, J. (1992), "A power primer," *Psychological Bulletin*, 112(1): 155–159.

Ellis, P.D., (2010a) "Effect sizes and the interpretation of research results in international business," *Journal of International Business Studies*, 41(9): 1581–1588.

Ellis, P.D. (2010b), *The Essential Guide to Effect Sizes: An Introduction to Statistical Power, Meta-Analysis and the Interpretation of Research Results*, Cambridge University Press.

Faul, F., E. Erdfelder, A.G. Lang, and A. Buchner (2007), "G*Power 3: A flexible statistical power analysis program for the social, behavioral, and biomedical sciences," *Behavior Research Methods*, 39(2): 175–191.

Faul, F., E., Erdfelder, A., Buchner, and A.G. Lang (2009), "Statistical power analyses using G*Power 3.1: Tests for correlation and regression analyses," *Behavior Research Methods*, 41: 1149–1160.

Fisher, R.A. (1925), *Statistical Methods for Research Workers.* Edinburgh: Oliver and Boyd.

Green, S.B. (1991), "How many subjects does it take to do a regression analysis?" *Multivariate Behavioral Research*, 26(3): 499–510.

Hung, K.H., F. Gu, and C.K. Yim (2007), "A social institutional approach to identifying generation cohorts in China with a comparison with American consumers," *Journal of International Business Studies*, 38(5): 836–853.

Ioannidis, J.P.A. (2005), "Why most published research findings are false," *PLoS Med*, website www.plosmedicine.org/article/info:doi/10.1371/jour nal.pmed.0020124, 696–701.

Kelley, K. and S.E. Maxwell (2008), "Sample size planning with applications to multiple regression: Power and accuracy for omnibus and targeted effects," in P. Alasuutari, L. Bickman, and J. Brannen (editors), *The Sage Handbook of Social Research Methods*, London: Sage, 166–192.

Kerr, N.L. (1998), "HARKing: Hypothesizing after the results are known," *Personality and Social Psychology Review*, 2(3): 196–217.

Kolata, G.B. (1981), "Drug found to help heart attack survivors," *Science*, 214(13): 774–775.

Kosciulek, J.F. and E.M. Szymanski (1993), "Statistical power analysis of rehabilitation research," *Rehabilitation Counseling Bulletin,* 36(4): 212–219.

Kroll, R.M. and L.J. Chase (1975), "Communication disorders: A power analytic assessment of recent research," *Journal of Communication Disorders*, 8(3): 237–247.

Lindsay, R.M. (1993), "Incorporating statistical power into the test of significance procedure: A methodological and empirical inquiry," *Behavioral Research in Accounting*, 5: 211–236.

Magnusson, P., D.W. Baack, S. Zdravkovic, K.M. Staub, and L.S. Amine (2008), "Meta-analysis of cultural differences: Another slice at the apple," *International Business Review*, 17(5): 520–532.

Mazen, A.M., L.A. Graf, C.E. Kellogg, and M. Hemmasi (1987), "Statistical power in contemporary management research," *Academy of Management Journal,* 30(2): 369–380.

McSwain, D.N. (2004), "Assessment of statistical power in contemporary accounting information systems research," *Journal of Accounting and Finance Research,* 12(7): 100–108.

Mone, M.A., G.C. Mueller, and W. Mauland (1996), "The perceptions and usage of statistical power in applied psychology and management research," *Personnel Psychology,* 49(1): 103–120.

Orme, J.G. and T.D. Combs-Orme (1986), "Statistical power and Type II errors in social work research," *Social Work Research and Abstracts,* 22(3): 3–10.

Reus, T.H. and D. Rottig (2009), "Meta-analyses of international joint venture performance determinants: Evidence for theory, artifacts and the unique context of China," *Management International Review,* 49(5): 607–640.

Rossi J.S. (1990), "Statistical power of psychological research: What have we gained in 20 years?" *Journal of Consulting and Clinical Psychology,* 58(5): 646–656.

Sawyer, A.G. and A.D. Ball (1981), "Statistical power and effect size in marketing research," *Journal of Marketing Research,* 18(3): 275–290.

Singh, J. (2007), "Asymmetry of knowledge spillovers between MNCs and host country firms," *Journal of International Business Studies,* 38(5): 764–786.

Sedlmeier, P. and G. Gigerenzer (1989), "Do studies of statistical power have an effect on the power of studies?" *Psychological Bulletin*, 105(2): 309–316.

Shoham, A. (2003), "Standardization of international strategy and export performance: A meta-analysis," in E. Kaynak (ed.) *Strategic Global Marketing: Issues and Trends*. Haworth Press: 97–120.

Tihanyi, L., D.A. Griffith, and C.J. Russell (2005), "The effect of cultural distance on entry mode choice, international diversification, and MNE performance: A meta-analysis," *Journal of International Business Studies*, 36(3): 270–283.

Zhao, H.X., Y.D. Luo, and T.W. Suh (2004), "Transaction cost determinants and ownership-based entry mode choice: A meta-analytical review," *Journal of International Business Studies*, 35(6): 524–544.

Zumbo, B.D. and A.M. Hubley (1998), "A note on misconceptions concerning prospective and retrospective power," *The Statistician*, 47 (Part2): 385–388.

META-
ANALYSIS
MADE EASY

How to Draw Definitive Conclusions from
Inconclusive Studies and Find Untapped
Gold Mines for Further Research!

Mad
Methods
.co

PAUL D. ELLIS

"Scientists have known for centuries that a single study will not resolve a major issue. Indeed, a small sample study will not even resolve a minor issue. Thus, the foundation of science is the cumulation of knowledge from the results of many studies."

— Hunter and Schmidt (1990: 13)

Why do I need this book?

This is a book for those preparing to start research projects. Whether you are a doctoral candidate or a full-chair professor, you may be asking questions like: How do I draw conclusions from inconclusive studies? How can I identify fruitful avenues for further research? How big a sample do I need to have a fair chance of detecting the effects I am seeking? This book will provide you with the tools you need to start answering these sorts of questions.

If you are a quantitative researcher, it's essential that you know something about meta-analysis. Now you could spend $80 on some brick of a book that contains more Greek than English and which you'll never read, or you could read this jargon-free introduction. You could sign up for a few classes, or you could spend an hour reading this book.

The examples in this book have been proven in the field and the classroom. They work. If you need to know about meta-analysis in a hurry, you won't find a better starting point.

Five reasons to read this book

There are at least five reasons why quantitative researchers should be familiar with meta-analysis:

1. Meta-analyses, in contrast with traditional narrative summaries or literature reviews, can bring order to a large and disparate set of studies. Meta-analyses are a powerful tool for establishing evidentiary benchmarks, even when prior research has been inconclusive.

2. A meta-analysis informs research by providing estimates of effect size that are essential to prospective analyses of statistical power. Want to know how many subjects you need for your own study? A meta-analysis of past research gives you the best estimates of effect size.

3. Effect size estimates generated by meta-analyses provide nonzero benchmarks against which research results can be compared. Meta-analysis thus provides researchers with more informed interpretation scenarios than merely assessing the likelihood of a null hypothesis.

4. A well-designed meta-analysis can examine contextual and other moderators that could not be easily tested in an individual study. The assessment of moderator effects is a powerful feature of meta-analysis as it can lead to new and unexpected discoveries.

5. Perhaps the most intriguing feature of meta-analysis is the process can lead to new hypotheses and promote theory development. Meta-analysis should not be seen as the culmination of past research, but as a doorway to further avenues of enquiry.

Who wrote this book?

I'm the inventor of meta-analysis. Actually, I'm not. Not by a long shot. But for a few weeks I thought I was.

I'm kind of embarrassed to admit this, but for a short time in my life I thought I had discovered meta-analysis. It happened about twenty years ago while attending a conference in Murcia, Spain. It was a warm afternoon and my mind drifting towards a siesta. I was thinking about effect sizes when I was struck by a bolt of lightning. "If we pooled effect size estimates from different studies, we could come up with an average estimate that was more accurate than any of the individual estimates."

Eureka! The opportunity was so obvious, I couldn't believe no one had thought of this before.

"What's more, we could weigh each estimate by the quality of the study from which it was obtained." It was a genius idea. If there was a Nobel Prize for research methods, I was going to get it!

Sadly, my euphoria lasted just as long as it took to learn of Gene Glass and Mary Lee Smith. Turns out Glass and Smith had beaten me by 30 years.

Although no one knows exactly who first came up with the idea of meta-analysis, Glass and Smith are widely acknowledged as pioneers for their seminal study of psychotherapy treatments (Glass 1976; Smith and Glass 1977). Wanting to know whether psychotherapy is beneficial, Glass and Smith set out to collect all the available evidence. They analyzed 833 effects obtained from 375 studies and found that psychotherapy works. This was great news for psychologists, but even better news was their novel technique of quantitatively pooling and analyzing the results of past research.

Glass and Smith's meta-analytic innovation sparked a revolution. In no time at all, meta-analyses were being used to examine all sorts of unresolved issues, particularly in the field of psychology. Meta-analysis had arrived.

I came to the party late, but better late than never. Learning how to think meta-analytically completely changed the way I looked at past research. I now had a tool far superior to the standard lit. review. I couldn't wait to try my hand at my first meta-analysis.

I was both thrilled to discover meta-analysis and saddened that I hadn't learned this stuff sooner. None of my methods teachers had said anything about it. I scanned the methods books on my shelves. The texts that did mention meta-analysis struck me as un-necessarily dense and hard to read.

Rather than curse the darkness I decided to light a candle. I wrote my own textbook, *The Essential Guide to Effect Sizes: Statistical Power, Meta-Analysis, and the Interpretation of Research Results*. It's a comprehensive yet jargon-free introduction to the largely ignored subject of effect sizes and their role in meta- and statistical power analyses.

When my book came out, I set up a website called www.effectsizefaq.com. The site has helpful tips and tricks along with links to useful resources. The site has proven popular with researchers attracting millions of page views.

By monitoring traffic stats, I have discovered that researchers and students are looking for straight-forward answers to three important questions:

(1) What is an effect size?
(2) How do I calculate the statistical power of my study?
(3) How do I draw definitive conclusions from inconclusive studies?

The book you are reading answers the third question. Two other books in the MadMethods series, *Effect Size Matters* and *Statistical Power Trip*, answer the first and second questions respectively. If you are unfamiliar with the concept of effect sizes, I recommend reading the first book before diving into this one. A good understanding of effect sizes and how to measure them is an essential precursor to meta-analysis. And if you wish to learn how to use effect sizes to design studies with sufficient power to detect them, the second book shows you how. (Value tip: You get three-books-in-one for a low price in the omnibus version.)

Why did I write these little books when I have already written a perfectly good text? Because students are poor and researchers are busy. You probably don't have six months to come to grips with these new subjects. You just want the short version. Your attitude is, *Just show me how!*

Your wish is granted.

This book is a quick and easy introduction to the subject of meta-analysis. By the time you're done reading it, you should be able to conduct a basic meta-analysis and recognize some of the pitfalls that undermine them.

Paul D. Ellis

Two ways to summarize past research

Research is cumulative in nature. At least, it's meant to be. But how often have you read the literature on a certain topic and come away scratching your head? "Study A reported a strong link between X and Y, Study B said there was no link, and Study C said the link ran in the opposite direction."

What do you do with disparate results? You conclude that a lack of consensus indicates a need for further research, so you do your own study. You get a result similar to Study C. "Hooray. My study found the same thing as that study. Progress!" But you can't help wondering what to do with the contrary results of Studies A and B.

Ideally, the results from different studies ought to line up. With each replication, we should be increasingly confident of the generalizability of emerging findings. But often what happens is the researcher is faced with the daunting task of making sense of disparate results.

This happened to me when I was a young researcher. At the time, I was interested in the relationship between market orientation and business performance. Is there one? You would expect so. Firms that are customer oriented ought to perform better, right? I surveyed the literature and what I found is summarized in Table 1.

Table 1: Market orientation research

Date	Country	Finding
1990	USA	strong
1993	USA	strong
1993	UK	weak
1995	UK	none
1995	New Zealand	none
1996	USA	strong
1998	Hong Kong	weak
2000	Korea	weak
2000	Germany	strong
2001	Australia	moderate
2001	India	strong

The beautiful thing about this body of work, is there is a lot of research measuring a common relationship or effect. The annoying thing is the results don't converge. Some studies say market orientation has a strong effect on performance; others say there is no effect. Which is it? Does market orientation affect performance or doesn't it? Why, after all this work, do we not have a straight answer to this question?

The fault lies not in the research, but in my summary of it. On what basis did I decide some results were strong, weak, or non-existent? It also appears that I gave every study equal weight, but was this fair? Surely a result drawn from a large sample deserves more weight than a result drawn from a small one, but I made no such distinction.

And herein lies the problem with the standard literature review, a.k.a., the narrative review.

What's wrong with narrative reviews?

There are two ways to review past research; a qualitative approach, also known as a narrative review, and a quantitative approach, also known as meta-analysis. Most PhD students and junior academics are familiar with the first approach. When beginning a study they collect all the relevant research, and then they try to make sense of it. They might attempt a short summary of past results. "Study A found this. Study B found that." Or they might create a table like the one above. In either case, definitive conclusions will be hard to draw because narrative summaries suffer from several inherent failings. First, they provide only a broad-brushed survey of extant work. Past results may be classified as "strong" or "weak" but what makes them so? Who decides? If a study reported a non-result, was that because there was no effect to detect or because the study lacked the power to detect it?

Second, narrative reviews typically fail to discriminate between studies done well and those done poorly. What are we to do with outlier studies? Do we treat them the same? Do we pretend we didn't see them? And what makes a study an outlier anyway?

Worst of all, narrative summaries are prone to researcher bias. How can we be sure the researcher has surveyed the entire field? Have they included unpublished studies? Were they thorough? And what have they done with awkward or contrary findings? Were they honest?

Reviewing past research is essential if we are to circumscribe the boundaries of existing knowledge and avoiding repeating past mistakes. But qualitative summaries of extant work are inherently limited. A far superior approach is to evaluate research using a quantitative approach or meta-analysis.

What is meta-analysis?

Meta-analysis is the statistical analysis of statistical analyses. Meta-analysis combines and compares the findings of different studies such that each study comprises an independent observation in the final sample of effect sizes.

Meta-analysis is quantitative in the sense that each study in the sample contributes a number, namely, a study-specific estimate of the effect size. We are not interested in whether the study's authors thought their results were strong or weak. They can keep their conclusions. We just want to see their evidence.

You may be wondering about effect sizes. An effect is simply an outcome, a result, a reaction, or a change in Y brought about by a change in X. An effect size refers to the magnitude of an outcome as it occurs, or would be found, in nature or in a population.

For instance, you may be interested in the effect of a vaccine on an infectious disease, or a policy change on presidential approval ratings, or a new strain of cereal on crop yields. An effect exists, or doesn't exist, out there, in the real world. When a scientist looks for evidence of the effect in a sample, they end up with an *estimate* of the effect size.

The estimate is the thing.

An effect size estimate will be more or less accurate depending on a variety of factors. How well was it measured? How representative was the sample? That sort of thing. The job of the scientist is to accurately estimate the size of the effect. In contrast, the job of the meta-analyst is to combine all the estimates obtained in different studies to come up with an average estimate. If the meta-analyst does their job well, their weighted mean estimate will be an accurate estimate of the true effect size.

I hope you are beginning to understand the value of a good meta-analysis. While a narrative review may leave you with more questions than answers, a good meta-analysis will deliver a very precise answer to the question everyone has been searching for, namely, *how big is the effect size?*

Why meta-analysis rocks

The chief attraction of meta-analysis is that it offers a framework for a scientifically rigorous accumulation of extant research findings. By doing meta-analysis we hope to identify the conclusions that would've been reached had the data from all the independent studies been collected in one big study.

When I "discovered" meta-analysis, I felt like I had found a gold mine. That's because my field, international business, is one big mess of studies done on a variety of topics in a variety of settings using a variety of methods. Before meta-analysis, I saw the mess; after meta-analysis, I saw unlimited opportunity. I will tell you about my first meta-analysis, and the surprising results it generated, below. But first, we need to ask…

What are the ingredients for good meta-analysis?

You have collected all the relevant research on a particular topic, and you want to summarize the results. You know narrative reviews tend to be flawed. Can you run a meta-analysis instead? It depends.

Not every body of work is amenable to meta-analysis. Meta-analysis requires that findings must be both (a) conceptually comparable and configured in (b) statistically equivalent forms (Lipsey and Wilson 2001).

Are the studies in your sample measuring essentially the same thing in essentially the same way? Or are they comparing apples with oranges?

In the market orientation example I gave you earlier, I neglected to mention that there are two ways to measure market orientation. Because two tools were devised by different authors at around the same time, the research can be divided into two groups depending on which tool they used; tool 1 or tool 2. Does this mean we cannot combine the results of these studies? Not necessarily.

In fact, the use of different measures can provide the meta-analyst with a unique opportunity to compare the effect of different measurement procedures. We'll return to this point below.

The second requirement for meta-analysis is the findings must be statistically equivalent. Is it possible to determine a common measure of effect size across studies? How do we compare studies that variously report *t*-tests, Chi-square, correlations, path coefficients, phi-coefficients, etc.? If studies report results in different metrics, the only way we can compare the results is by converting them all into a common measure of effect size.[14]

If the research you wish to review meets these two requirements of being conceptually comparable and statistically equivalent, you can conduct meta-analysis.

---

[14] Some procedures for doing this are covered in my MadMethods book *Effect Size Matters*.

How to bake a cake: meta-analysis in 4 easy steps

A while ago I began a graduate methods class with a question. "How many of you have done a meta-analysis."

No hands went up.

"How many of you believe you will have completed your first meta-analysis before our class is done?" A few uncertain hands went up, but most stayed down.

Meta-analysis sounds hard but it's actually straightforward. It's like baking cake. As long as you stick to the recipe, you'll end up with something good.

Let me prove this by using the example I use in the classroom.

To keep things simple, let's imagine we are interested in a body of research consisting of four studies (see Table 2).

Table 2: Four fictitious studies

	Study 1	Study 2	Study 3	Study 4
r	0.453	0.321	0.301	0.075
p	<0.001	0.049	0.033	0.722
n	87	38	50	25

Here we have four studies each reporting estimates of an effect size in the correlational metric. (The numbers in this example come from Field (1999).) Three of the studies reported a statistically significant result ($p < .05$), but one did not. However, we care nothing for these p-values. They are irrelevant to our meta-analysis. We are primarily interested in the individual effect size estimates (r) and the sample sizes (N) from which they were obtained.

The primary purpose of a meta-analysis is to calculate an estimate of the population effect size based on the individual sample-based estimates. The easiest way to do that is to average the correlations.

Summing the correlations in Table 1 and dividing by the number of samples (four) gives an average r of 0.288. This is our mean effect size, and the first thing we notice about it is that it is appreciably lower than three of the four observed correlation coefficients.

This demonstrates how the simple average can be biased.

In our dataset, a very small correlation coefficient was reported in Study 4. Although this estimate came from a small sample, it was given equal weight with the estimates obtained from larger samples. This is hardly ideal and it probably compromised our result. Why? Because larger samples return better effect size estimates than smaller ones.

One solution to this problem is to calculate a weighted average using this formula from Hunter and Schmidt (1990):

$$\bar{r} = \frac{\sum n_i r_i}{\sum n_i}$$

The Greek letter sigma means sum. (I promise you this is one of the few times any Greek symbols will appear in this book!) We multiply each study's effect size estimate (r) by the sample size (n), sum the lot, then divide the result by the sum of the four sample sizes. This gives us a weighted mean effect size (or r-bar) as follows:

$$= \frac{(87 \times 0.453) + (38 \times 0.321) + (50 \times 0.301) + (25 \times 0.075)}{87 + 38 + 50 + 25}$$

$$= \frac{68.53}{200}$$

$$= 0.343$$

The weighted mean effect size (0.343) is larger than the unweighted one (0.288). Is this a better estimate of the population effect size? Most definitely. By giving more weight to the larger samples, we have reduced the contaminating effects of sampling error.

But wait, there's more!

The effect size estimates returned in each study are also affected by the reliability or internal consistency of the measures used. Studies reporting low measurement reliability generate estimates that are lower than the true or population effect size on account of noisy measures.

So let us introduce one more piece of information into the analysis. Cronbach's alpha (α) is routinely reported in studies measuring variables with multi-item scales. In Table 3 below, the alpha obtained from each study is reported in the second to last row.

Table 3: Four corrected effect sizes

	Study 1	Study 2	Study 3	Study 4
r	0.453	0.321	0.301	0.075
n	87	38	50	25
α	0.94	0.70	-	0.82
Corrected ES	*0.467*	*0.384*	*0.332*	*0.083*

We correct for measurement error by dividing each effect size (r) by the square root of the reliability of the measurement instrument (α). For studies failing to report reliabilities, such as Study 3, we substitute the mean reliability observed across the whole dataset. Crunching the numbers gives the corrected effect sizes we see in the bottom row of Table 3. Plugging these into the same equation above gives us a weighted mean effect size corrected for measurement error, as follows:

$$= \frac{(87 \times 0.467) + (38 \times 0.384) + (50 \times 0.332) + (25 \times 0.083)}{87 + 38 + 50 + 25}$$

$$= \frac{73.90}{200}$$

$$= 0.369$$

Because we have pooled the results of past research, we can be reasonably confident that our weighted mean effect size of $r = 0.369$ is closer to the true population effect size, than any of the estimates obtained in the four individual studies.

Which is pretty cool.

If you have managed to follow along—it wasn't that hard, was it?—congratulations! You've just learned how to do a meta-analysis.

Actually, you have learned how to do one type of meta-analysis. There are several meta-analytic methods, but two dominate. The Coke and Pepsi of meta-analysis, if you like, are the rival methods developed by Hunter and Schmidt (2000) and by Hedges (1981, 2007). The method we have just learned is the Hunter and Schmidt method. If you would like to learn about the others, check out any good meta-analysis textbook. And if you would like more practice on crunching the numbers, check out the exercises in the Appendix.

Now that you've learned how to do a basic meta-analytic procedures, let me illustrate the process using an example based on my first published meta-analysis (Ellis, 2006). In my meta-analysis, I was interested in the effect of a market orientation on performance. In the business literature, there is a large body of research that says being customer focused and so forth either has a strong effect or no effect on business performance. A narrative review of this research will give you no clear conclusion, but can a meta-analysis do better?

To answer this question, I followed four steps:

(i)   compile a set of effect size estimates
(ii)   calculate a weighted mean effect size
(iii) calculate a confidence interval for the mean effect size
(iv)   interpret the results

Step 1: Compile a set of effect sizes

Remember, a meta-analysis can only be done on research that is conceptually comparable and statistically equivalent. Market orientation research fits both criteria as it is a well-defined body of work examining the same relationship (the effect of market orientation on performance) with results usually reported in the correlational metric.

While a narrative review may be selective, a good meta-analysis ought to be thorough. Every estimate of the effect size should be included. In my case, I began by conducting a census of all the relevant research. I systematically searched databases relevant to my field for empirical articles published from 1990 to 2004, and I manually scanned published references.

My initial search yielded 202 journal articles plus four soon-to-be-published studies. I was so dazzled by the large number of studies I had found, that I made my first mistake. I did not consider *unpublished* studies. Full disclosure: This means my analysis may have been compromised by the availability bias. More on this in Part B.

My starting point (the 206 papers) led me to identify a smaller number of independent studies. To be included in my meta-analysis, each study had to report a sample size and some measure of effect size. Since most of the studies in my database reported a correlational measure of effect size, I adopted r as the effect size of interest. If a study did not report zero-order correlations or provide statistics which could be converted to a correlation, I wrote to the authors to solicit correlations directly.

(Tip for scholars: In your descriptive stats, always report your correlation matrix. Even if your results are statistically nonsignificant, meta-analysts will want to see them.)

You don't need a special statistical program to conduct a meta-analysis. A well laid-out spreadsheet will suffice. In my spreadsheet, each row corresponded to a single study, while each column contained quantitative details about the studies. From each study I recorded the effect size, the sample size, and the type of tool used to measure market orientation. I also recorded the reliability of the measurement tool (Cronbach's alpha), and the type of performance variables reported. I also recorded some contextual information about each study, such as where it was done.

In my study, the outcome or dependent variable was performance. Performance can be a tricky beast to measure. In my dataset a variety of measures had been adopted and it was important to take these differences into account. Consequently, I coded studies according to the scope of their performance measure (i.e., business-level measures such as profits or market-specific measures such as customer satisfaction) and the type of measures used (i.e., objective versus subjective assessments).

Any study that reported an effect size more than 2.5 standard deviations from the combined mean was considered an outlier and dropped from the meta-analysis. (One study was deleted.) When I was done compiling my dataset, I had 58 useable studies. Collectively these studies reported data collected from 14,586 firms based in 28 different countries.

Step 2: Calculate a weighted mean effect size

At the end of Step 1, I had a set of 58 effect size estimates, drawn from different studies. However, these estimates were not directly comparable on account of differences in sample size and measurement reliability. To attenuate the effects of sampling and measurement error, effect size estimates were divided by the square root of the reliability of the measurement instrument and weighted by the size of the sample from which they were obtained. For studies failing to report reliabilities, a mean reliability figure was substituted.

After correcting for sample size and measurement error, I was able to calculate a weighted mean effect size of $r = 0.26$. (It's a simple number, but it represents a lot of work.) What does my result mean? While narrative summaries of past research give ambiguous conclusions, examining the effect sizes directly leads to the unequivocal conclusion that market orientation is positively related to business performance, just as you would expect.

So far, so good. But can we say more? And how confident are we that our estimate of the effect size is close to the true effect size? To answer that question, I needed to...

Step 3: Calculate the confidence interval for the weighted mean

The end result of a meta-analysis is a single estimate of the population effect size. (That doesn't sound like much, but you can do a lot with that number as we will see in Part B.) How do we know if our estimate — the weighted mean — is any good?

To answer that question, we can convert the result to a z score then determine whether the probability of obtaining a score of this size is less than .05, or we can calculate a 95 percent confidence interval. In meta-analysis, the latter approach is more common.

A confidence interval establishes the degree of precision in the estimate of the mean effect size. Unlike a standard test of statistical significance, confidence intervals are centered on observed values rather than the hypothetical value of a null hypothesis.

With a confidence interval, we are looking for two things. First, does the range of the interval include 0? A 95% confidence interval that excludes 0 puts the odds of $p = 0$ beyond reasonable possibility and indicates that the mean effect size is statistically significant at $\alpha = .05$.

Second, is the interval narrow or wide? Narrow is better and more precise. Confidence intervals will be wider for distributions that are heterogeneous, that is, where two or more population means have been combined into a single estimate of mean effect size.

To calculate a confidence interval for a mean effect size, we need to know the standard error (SE) or (v_r) variance of the mean effect size. This can be found by multiplying the square of the difference between each effect size estimate and the mean by the sample size, summing the lot, then dividing the result by the total sample size. Hunter and Schmidt (1990) provide the equation:

$$v_{\cdot_r} = \frac{\sum n_i (r_i - \bar{r})^2}{\sum n_i}$$

In my market orientation study the variance or SE was 0.0087. To calculate the upper and lower bounds of my confidence interval, I multiplied the SE by the critical value of the z-distribution (1.96 when α = .05), then subtracted (or added) the result to the mean effect size (0.263) to determine the lower (or upper) bounds of the confidence interval:

$$\text{Confidence interval} = \bar{r} \pm 1.96\, SE_{\bar{r}}$$

Doing this gave me a CI95 of 0.246—0.280. Since this range excluded zero, I concluded that my result was statistically significant.

Step 4: Interpret the results

The final step in any analysis is to interpret the results. We do this by asking, what do the results mean and for whom? If Step 3 tells us whether a result is statistically significant, then Step 4 is concerned with the practical or substantive significance of the result.

Once upon a time, any meta-analysis that was done well stood a decent chance of getting published. Provided you did a fair job collecting and coding studies, knew how to crunch the numbers, you'd get a hit. Those days are long gone. Now editors expect more. Consider the following advice which comes from the editor of the prestigious *Academy of Management Journal*:

> AMJ will publish meta-analyses that fulfil the promise of the method's champions: advancing theoretical knowledge. A meta-analysis that merely tallies the existing literature quantitatively but provides no new insights into the nature of the relationships so tallied will not be favored. A meta-analysis that sheds new light on how or why a relationship or set of relationships occurs should be (re)viewed favorably. (Eden 2002: 844)

Identifying the contribution to theory is just one part of the interpretation challenge. Increasingly, editors want answer to questions like these: Are the results reported in non-arbitrary metrics that can be understood by nonspecialists? What is the context of this effect? Who is affected or who potentially could be affected by this result and why does it matter? What is the net contribution to knowledge? Does this result confirm or disconfirm what was already known or suspected? Is this result small, medium, or large?

I discuss the interpretation challenge in my MadMethods book *Effect Size Matters*, and I won't repeat that material here. However, it is worth noting that meta-analyses offer unique interpretation opportunities. The meta-analyst, with her big picture of the data, can see things that were missed in the individual studies. How meta-analysis leads to the discovery of new knowledge is the subject of Part B.

Intermission

In Part A our focus was on the pooling of effect size estimates from prior research. One of the reasons we collect and combine these estimates is to delineate the boundaries of existing knowledge. Another reason is to identify potentially interesting avenues for further exploration.

If the question in Part A was, "what do we know?" the question we now turn to in Part B is, "where do we go from here?"

Meta-analysis and the discovery of new knowledge

A good meta-analysis represents more than the culmination of a stream of research and is a stepping stone to new and exciting avenues of research and theory development.

Meta-analysis contributes to theory by making sense of the literature and by examining the influence of contextual moderators.

What is a moderator?

A moderator is a third variable that affects or moderates the relationship between an X and Y. In my market orientation meta-analysis, I examined a number of measurement- and contextual-moderators.

Recall that there are two ways or tools for measuring market orientation. By coding studies on the basis of which tool they used, I was able to assess whether the choice of measurement tool had any effect on the central relationship.

It did.[15]

And since there are different ways of measuring performance, I was able to test for that as well. Specifically, I coded tests based on whether they assessed performance using objective or subjective measures. Crunching the numbers revealed market orientation had a stronger correlation with the latter.

Measurement moderators are interesting in that they inform prospective analyses of statistical power and steer future researchers towards particular measurement tools, but where meta-analysis really shines is in the analysis of contextual moderators.

My meta-analysis was based on 58 separate studies conducted in 28 different countries. This offered me a unique opportunity to see whether effect sizes were affected by things like economic development and culture. Essentially, I wanted to know whether the market orientation — performance relationship is

---

[15] If you're a business researcher, you may be interested to learn that studies measuring market orientation using items inspired by Kohli, Jaworski and Kumar's (1993) MARKOR scale returned significantly higher effect sizes (r = .32, CI = .29 — .36) than those inspired by Narver and Slater's (1990) MKTOR instrument (r = .25, CI = .23 — .27).

universal or whether it's affected by local market conditions. I had good reasons for suspecting the effect of a market orientation might be ameliorated by the sort of country you live in.

Consider two businesses that are equally market oriented. Both are highly focused on their customers and competitors. However, the first business is located in a free market economy characterized by buyers' markets and intense competition, while the second is located in a developing economy characterized by sellers' markets and rapid growth. Do these location differences affect the potency of each firm's market orientation?

That's what I wanted to find out.

To do this I coded each study according to a number of contextual or country-specific variables. These included the cultural distance from the U.S., and the size and economic development of the home economy at the time of data collection. (If you want to know how I quantified these variables, see Ellis (2006).)

I won't bore you with the details, but my findings confirmed my suspicion that effect sizes were larger

241

when measured in mature, western markets, and relatively small in underdeveloped economies that are culturally distant from the US (see Table 4).

Table 4: Mean effect sizes for moderator sub-groups in Ellis (2006)

Contextual moderators		*n*	Corrected *r*	95% CI
Culture	West	37	0.285	0.262 - 0.307
	East	19	0.228	0.201 - 0.255
Cultural dist.	Low	28	0.286	0.262 - 0.309
from U.S.	High	29	0.236	0.212 - 0.261
Market size	Small	29	0.222	0.200 - 0.244
	Large	29	0.322	0.295 - 0.348
Economic	Developing	28	0.228	0.206 - 0.251
development	Mature	30	0.308	0.282 - 0.333

For an international business researcher, this was an intriguing finding, pregnant with possibilities. But here's the thing: this discovery was made without collecting any primary data.

If I had designed a multi-country study to search for these effects, it would have been prohibitively expensive. (Fourteen thousand firms in 28 countries!) But obtaining this knowledge required nothing more than access to prior research, an Excel spreadsheet, and a little meta-analytic thinking.

How to ruin a meta-analysis

If you've come this far, you may be thinking "Meta-analyses are awesome," and you're not wrong. But like any tool, they can be abused and misused.

Now that I have impressed you with the story of my first meta-analysis, it's time to 'fess up and tell you what I got wrong. Although it wasn't a bad first attempt, in hindsight I could have done some things better.

There are several ways to scuttle a meta-analysis, but the greatest danger may be that presented by the exclusion of relevant research.[16] By design, a meta-analyst will seek to include all estimates of an effect size in their study. To the degree that some estimates are missed, the meta-analytic results may be compromised by an availability bias.

---

[16] Other sources of bias, which I cover in *The Essential Guide to Effect Sizes*, are the inclusion of false results, the use of inappropriate statistical models, and running meta-analyses with insufficient statistical power.

What is an availability bias?

An availability bias arises when effect size estimates obtained from studies which are readily available (e.g., published studies, conference papers) differ from those obtained from studies which are less accessible (e.g., unpublished studies, studies written in foreign languages).

I said that running a meta-analysis is as easy as baking a cake. It is, provided you have all the ingredients. A more accurate analogy might be to say that meta-analysis is like baking a cake when some of the ingredients are hard to find. Miss key ingredients and you could ruin your cake.

Imagine ten scientists all investigating the same effect. Five of them get statistically significant results and go on to publish their findings. However, the other five scientists leave their nonsignificant results filed away and unpublished. What can we say about these ten studies?

All things being equal, the five published studies probably found larger effect sizes than the unpublished ones. This happens because statistical significance is determined by several variables, one of which is the effect size. Since journals are in the habit of publishing studies that found something as opposed to studies that found nothing, studies which find larger effects are more likely to get published than studies which find smaller ones. And this is bad news for meta-analysts.

Actually, it's bad news for everyone.

When results don't pan out, research goes unreported. "I didn't get a good p-value. No editor will want to see this." No editor won't, but a meta-analyst will.

Your carefully conducted study contains a legitimate estimate of an effect size and that will always be of interest to other researchers, regardless of the results of statistical significance tests.

An availability bias can emerge in a variety of ways. The first source of an availability bias is the so-called **file drawer problem** which arises when researchers do nothing with their results. Got an unexpected or nonsignificant result? Don't hide it. Report it. If you can't get it in a journal, present it as a conference paper. At the very least, put it on your website and make it publicly available.

Related to the file drawer problem is the **reporting bias** which arises when researchers only report some of their findings.

Say you run four tests and get two statistically significant results. If you only publish the two "good" results while filing away the others, you will inadvertently contribute to an availability bias and the inflation in effect sizes obtained in subsequent meta-analyses. Again, this happens because statistical significance is related to effect size. Small effects are less likely to generate statistically significant results. But this doesn't mean they're invalid, useless, or wrong. In the right context, small effects can be profoundly important.

In addition to researchers, editors also limit the availability of research if they exhibit a preference for publishing statistically significant results. A **publication bias** emerges when statistically nonsignificant results obtained from methodologically sound studies lead to the nonpublication of those studies.

There is considerable evidence that this happens in practice (Coursol and Wagner, 1986). What does this mean for the meta-analyst? Base your study exclusively on published research, and you will likely end up with inflated estimates of the effect size.

Finally, there is the wonderfully-named **Tower of Babel bias** whereby results published in languages other than English are excluded from meta-analyses. There is research to show that non-native English speakers are more likely to submit to English-language journals when their results are "strong," meaning big and statistically significant, and are less likely to do so when their results are less impressive (Grégoire *et al.*, 1995).

How to deal with an availability bias?

A good meta-analysis will include every estimate of a particular effect size, regardless of whether the estimate is small or large, positive or negative, published or filed away. But the presence of an availability bias undermines this goal.

What can the meta-analyst do? Obviously, they need to make every effort to collect those estimates. Getting estimates from published research is easy; getting estimates which have gone unreported or have been filed away is tricky.

A good meta-analyst will put out calls on discussion boards and research groups. They will reach out to scholars known to be working in the area. They may not be able to collect every unreported result, but even some will be better than none.

A meta-analyst who succeeds in collecting unpublished results can compare the mean estimates obtained from those results with those obtained from published results. This will enable them to quantify and mitigate the threat of the availability bias.

Another remedy is to calculate the "fail-safe N." The fail-safe N is the number of additional studies with contrary evidence (e.g., null results) that would be needed to overturn a meta-analytic conclusion. The aim is to make the fail-safe N as high as possible. The higher the N the more confidence we have in the meta-analysis.

Another way to quantify the threat of an availability bias is to create a funnel plot showing the distribution of effect sizes. A funnel plot is a scatter plot where each effect size estimate is placed on a XY graph where X corresponds to the effect size and Y corresponds to the sample size. The idea is that the precision of the estimates increases with sample size.

Relatively imprecise estimates obtained from small samples will be scattered widely along the bottom of the graph, while more precise estimates obtained from larger samples will be in a tighter bunch at the top of the graph. If you have collected a representative database of effect sizes, the dispersion of results will describe a funnel shape. However, the existence of an availability bias will render the plot asymmetrical.

I mentioned earlier than in my market orientation meta-analysis, I collected results from published studies and conference papers. I did not make any effort to collect unpublished results because it never occurred to me to do so. Hindsight is a wonderful thing. If I had been aware of the threat of an availability bias, I could have done something about it.

Better late than never. Figure 1 is a funnel plot I created specifically for this book. Each dot on the plot represents a study-specific estimate of the effect size, while the diamond represents the weighted mean obtained across the fifteen studies in this group. To reduce clutter, the plot only contains the subset of studies that used the first tool for measuring market orientation.

Figure 1: Funnel plot for Ellis (2006)

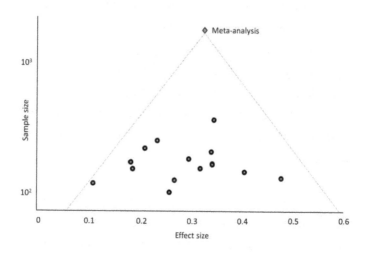

Does the scatterplot in Figure 1 appear symmetrical and funnel-shaped? It generally does. The widest spread of results appears along the bottom while results from larger studies are more closely bunched together at the top. This is what we would expect to see if there was little threat from an availability bias.

If we were being picky, we might argue that there is a bit of vacant space towards the lower right side of the funnel. But this space would have been occupied by studies returning large effect sizes, while the presence of an availability bias would suggest an absence of studies returning small ones.

No funnel plot is perfect, and mine is about as good as they come. Consequently, I can be reasonably confident that my dataset was not compromised by an availability bias.

Phew!

Enough about me and my brilliant meta-analysis. It's time to discuss someone else's meta-analysis, and this one is a doozy.

Meta-analysis and moon madness

Is mental health affected by the moon? It seems a strange question, but moon madness, has long been the stuff of folklore. (Have you ever noticed how the word *lunacy* derives from *luna*, the Latin word for moon?) Sceptics scoff at the association, but serious research has examined links between phases of the moon and various types of undesirable behaviour.

Scholars who subscribe to the "lunar effect" suspect that there may be an element of truth behind folk beliefs or that the beliefs create self-fulfilling prophecies. In either case, a number of hypotheses have been advanced to explore lunar-lunacy links: variations in moonlight may affect the pineal gland triggering unusual behaviour; criminals may prefer the darkness provided by a new moon; bodily fluids may be affected by the moon's gravitational pull, and so on.

Needless to say this work is considered highly controversial among psychologists. On the one side are those who argue that any positive findings are examples of Type I error, while on the other side are those who argue that failures to observe any lunar effect are examples of Type II error and underpowered research.

To settle this issue, Rotton and Kelly (1985) conducted a meta-analysis of 37 published studies investigating links between phases of the moon and outcomes such as homicides, suicides, psychiatric disturbances, admissions to mental institutions, and calls to crisis centers.

Interestingly, they found some statistically significant, though very small effects. However, they reasoned that these results may have been upwardly biased by a file drawer problem that is probably greater for lunar research than other fields of enquiry. If 100 scientists decided to test the lunar hypothesis and one happened to find a result, that particular scientist would be far more likely to get his paper published than the 99 who found nothing.

Rotton and Kelly also rejected a causal link on conceptual grounds arguing that the lunar hypothesis consistently fails the tests of replicability and predictability.

> Just as we cannot prove that werewolves, unicorns and other interesting creatures do not exist, we cannot prove that the moon does not influence behavior. However, the burden of proof lies with those who favour the lunar hypothesis. They will have to collect a great deal more—and better—data before they can reject the null hypothesis of no relation between phases of the moon and behaviour. (1985: 300)

The moon madness study highlights the overarching importance of careful interpretation. Rotton and Kelly found *something*—their meta-analysis detected some effects—but concluded their something was really nothing given the high likelihood of a large and confounding availability bias. Meta-analysis is a useful tool, but in science, replication is everything.

Thinking meta-analytically

Now that you have a basic grasp of the issues, you may be inspired to attempt a meta-analysis of your own. Go for it! But start by investing in a good text book. Although we have peeled away some of the mystery surrounding meta-analysis, this short guide should not be considered a substitute for comprehensive text.

If you have no interest in attempting a meta-analysis, hopefully you have at least learned the value of thinking meta-analytically. If so, you will no longer be swayed by authors' conclusions or vague statements of significance. When reading empirical literature, your mindset will be, "Show me the evidence, and let me decide for myself."

And thus we come full circle. To think meta-analytically requires some expectations regarding effect sizes and the ability to analyze statistical power. Like the legs on a stool, these three concepts are intimately related.

Author's note

If you enjoyed *Meta-Analysis Made Easy*, would you
mind posting a short customer review on Amazon?
Doing so will help others find this book.

Thank you!

Appendix: Bonus exercise

In my graduate methods class, I would give students three papers to read for the purposes of completing a simple meta-analysis. If you would like to try this exercise for yourself, the papers are (1) Langerak *et al.*, (2004), (2) Slater and Narver (2000), and (3) Selnes *et al.*, (1996).

- Task 1: Skim read the papers to fill in the gaps in the table below (sample size, Cronbach's alpha for the market orientation instrument (α), effect size (r), and corrected effect size)
- Task 2: Calculate a simple mean effect size
- Task 3: Calculate a weighted mean effect size
- Task 4: Calculate a weighted mean effect size corrected for measurement error

The answers are found on the following page.

Study	Setting	N	MO α	r	Perf.	Corrected ES
1	Netherlands				Org. perf.	
2	USA				ROI	
3a	Scandinavia				Subj. perf.	
3b	USA				Subj. perf.	

Answers to the exercise:

Task 1: Complete the table

Study	Sample N	MO α	r	Perf.	Corrected ES
1	126	0.84	0.33	Org. perf.	0.360
2	53 (SBUs)	0.77	0.362	ROI	0.413
3a	237 (SBUs)	0.89	0.21	Subj. perf.	0.223
3b	222 (SBUs)	0.89	0.34	Subj. perf.	0.360

Task 2: Calculate a simple mean effect size

$$\frac{0.33 + 0.362 + 0.21 + 0.34}{4} = 0.31$$

How do you feel about this result? Does it seem accurate?

In this simple approach, all studies are treated equally. But notice how the largest correlation was reported in the smallest study, while the smallest correlation was found in the largest sample.

Let us attenuate our mean effect size by weighting each correlation by the sample size on which it is based.

Task 3: Calculate Weighted Mean Effect Size

$$= \frac{(126 \times 0.33) + (53 \times 0.362) + (237 \times 0.21) + (222 \times 0.34)}{126 + 53 + 237 + 222}$$

$$= \frac{(41.58) + (19.19) + (49.77) + (75.48)}{638}$$

$$= 0.29$$

Task 4: Calculate Weighted Mean Corrected for Measurement Error

Redo Task 3 above using estimates of effect size that have been corrected for measurement error.

$$= \frac{(126 \times 0.36) + (53 \times 0.413) + (237 \times 0.223) + (222 \times 0.36)}{126 + 53 + 237 + 222}$$

$$= \frac{(45.36) + (21.89) + (52.85) + (79.92)}{638}$$

$$= 0.314$$

References

Coursol, A. and E.E. Wagner (1986), "Effect of positive findings on submission and acceptance rates: A note on meta-analysis bias," *Professional Psychology: Research and Practice,* 17(2): 136-137.

Eden, D. (2002), "Replication, meta-analysis, scientific progress, and *AMJ*'s publication policy," *Academy of Management Journal,* 45(5): 841–846.

Ellis, P.D. (2006), "Market orientation and performance: A meta-analysis and cross-national comparisons," *Journal of Management Studies,* 43(5): 1089–1107.

Field, A.P. (1999), "A bluffer's guide to meta-analysis I: Correlations," *Newsletter of the Mathematical, Statistical and computing section of the British Psychological Society,* 7 (1), 16–25.

Grégoire, G., F. Derderian, and J. LeLorier (1995), "Selecting the language of the publications included in a meta-analysis: Is there a Tower of Babel bias?" *Journal of Clinical Epidemiology,* 48(1): 159-163.

Glass, G. (1976), "Primary, secondary, and meta-analysis of research," *Educational Researcher* 5:3–8.

Hedges, L.V. (1981), "Distribution theory for Glass's estimator of effect size and related estimators," *Journal of Educational Statistics,* 6(2): 106–128.

Hedges, L.V. (2007), "Meta-analysis," in C.R. Rao and

S. Sinharay (2007), *Handbook of Statistics, Vol.26,* Amsterdam: Elsevier, 919–953.

Hunter, J.E. and F.L. Schmidt (1990) *Methods of Meta-Analysis,* Newbury Park, CA: Sage.

Hunter, J.E. and F.L. Schmidt (2000), "Fixed effects vs. random effects meta-analysis models: Implications for cumulative research knowledge," *International Journal of Selection and Assessment,* 8(4): 275–292.

Kohli, A.K., B.J. Jaworski and A. Kumar (1993), "MARKOR: A measure of market orientation," *Journal of Marketing Research,* 30 (November): 467-477.

Langerak, F., E.J. Hultink, and H.S.J. Robben (2004), "The impact of market orientation, product advantage and launch proficiency on new product performance and organizational performance," *The Journal of Product Innovation Management,* 21(2): 79-94.

Lipsey, M.W. and D.B. Wilson (2001) *Practical Meta-Analysis,* Thousand Oaks, CA: Sage.

Narver, J.C. and S.F. Slater (1990), "The effect of a market orientation on business profitability," *Journal of Marketing,* 54 (October): 20-35.

Rotton, J. and I.W. Kelly (1985), "Much ado about the full moon: A meta-analysis of lunar-lunacy research," *Psychological Bulletin,* 97(2): 286–306.

Selnes, F., B.J. Jaworski, and A.K. Kohli (1996), "Market orientation in United States and Scandinavian companies," *Scandinavian Journal of Management*, 12(2): 139-157.

Slater, S.F. and J.C. Narver (2000), "The positive effect of a market orientation on business profitability: A balanced replication," *Journal of Business Research*, 48(1): 69-73.

Smith, M.L. and G.V. Glass (1977), "Meta-analysis of psychotherapy outcome studies," *American Psychologist*, 32(9): 752–760.